A YANKEE REFORMER IN CHILE

A YANKEE REFORMER IN CHILE

THE LIFE & WORKS OF DAVID TRUMBULL

by Irven Paul

William Carey Library

533 HERMOSA STREET • SOUTH PASADENA, CALIF. 91030 • TEL. 213-682-2047

Framingham State College
Framingham, Massachusetts

©Copyright 1973 by the William Carey Library
All rights reserved.
No part of this book may be used or reproduced in any manner whatsoever without written permission, except in the case of brief quotations embodied in critical articles and reviews.

International Standard Book Number 0-87808-414-2
Library of Congress Catalog Number 72-94134

Published by the William Carey Library
533 Hermosa Street
South Pasadena, Calif. 91030
Telephone 213-682-2047

PRINTED IN THE UNITED STATES OF AMERICA

To

Horacio Gonzalez Contesse,

*Congenial Colleague and Contemporary
Agent of The Reformed Church in Chile*

CONTENTS

FOREWORD
PREFACE
ACKNOWLEDGEMENTS

CHAPTER 1.	THE NEW ENGLAND HERITAGE	1
CHAPTER 2.	FAMILY PORTRAIT	6
	Makers of History	19
CHAPTER 3.	EDUCATION AND CALL TO SERVICE	32
CHAPTER 4.	FORERUNNERS IN THE VALE OF PARADISE	45
	Latin American Precursors	47
	Anglo-Saxon Forerunners	50
CHAPTER 5.	THE REFORMED CHURCH IN THE WILDERNESS	61
CHAPTER 6.	AGENT OF THE EVANGELICAL MAGISTERIUM	67
	The Philosophy of Education in the Reformed Tradition	67
	The Blas Cuevas School	68
	The Artizan School	69
	La Escuela Popular (A School for the People)	72
	The Instituto Inglés (English Academy)	73
CHAPTER 7.	THE WORD OF GOD IS SPREAD ABROAD	75
	The Establishment of the Valparaiso Bible Society	79

CHAPTER 8.	THE GOSPEL IN THE REFORMED TRADITION	84
	The Splendor and Tragedy of Man	86
	Jesus Christ, Son of God, Savior	88
	The Church as the Gathered and Scattered People of God	90
	Keep the Unity of the Spirit (Ephesians 4:3)	92
	The Gospel in Terms of Emancipation	94
	The Gospel in Terms of Social Concern and Action	97
CHAPTER 9.	ADVOCATE OF CONSTITUTIONAL REFORMS	100
	The Secularization of the Cemeteries	102
CHAPTER 10.	MISSION ACCOMPLISHED	108
CHAPTER 11.	EPILOGUE	112
APPENDIX A.	ANCESTRAL GOSSIP	121
APPENDIX B.	A SEAMAN'S FRIEND	129
APPENDIX C.	LETTERS WRITTEN BY DAVID TRUMBULL	135
NOTES		138
BIBLIOGRAPHY		148

FOREWORD

Latin America, which was once a quiet backwater of the world's life, is now pushing more and more into the center stream. The rate of change accelerates constantly as the power of the main current takes hold. Many observers regard this continent as the arena for the greatest social changes in the world--and this is one arena where religion and religious bodies are very deeply involved in all that is happening.

In such a time it is increasingly important to understand how the changes began and from what sources they came. One source, though it may not be of the greatest importance, is still far more important than would be indicated by the attention it has received. This is the work of Protestant missionaries coming from North America and Europe. Much more needs to be known about the contributions which the early missionaries made to the first ferment of change in the old colonial society, which had existed in isolated stability for three hundred years. Their religious convictions and their social attitudes were part of a fresh wind blowing into that still air.

To anyone who will persue the following pages, it will become clear that the work of David Trumbull provided a particularly noteworthy example of the contributions made by the early Protestants. He manifested both the strong religious convictions and the social concerns that were theirs. To the present-day reader, accustomed to the more radical changes of this century, his teachings and activities may seem quite conservative. The changes he was primarily interested in were either strictly in the field of religious belief, or very closely connected to religious questions--changes such as the separation of church and state, the opening of non-confessional schools, the secularizing of cemeteries, and the granting of greater freedoms to religious minorities. Although today his program seems very limited, it was part of the process of opening up and liberalizing the continent, without which the changes of our time could not even have seen suggested.

There is another respect in which Trumbull can stand as a precursor of what is being called for today in South America. That is in his sense of identification with the people to whom he went. His final step of adopting Chilean citizenship shows that he was not willing to work from the top down or from outside in--but that he recognized, as is so often emphasized today, the necessity of being part of the people in order to make any change in their life. Trumbull's attitudes and way of working were in certain respects well ahead of his time.

The importance of the work which Dr. Paul has provided can be inferred from what has been said here. It is to be hoped that many of the growing body of people who are alert to, and concerned about, South America today will benefit from reading this account of one of the significant figures of church life on that continent.

CHARLES W. FORMAN
Professor of Missions
The Divinity School
Yale University

PREFACE

More than a half century ago Dr. Robert E. Speer, Secretary of the Presbyterian Board of Foreign Missions, wrote a chapter on the "Life and Works of David Trumbull" in his book *Studies of Missionary Leadership*.

The present biographical narrative purports to be an enlargement of the former portrait of the missionary statesman by viewing his life and works in the historical perspective of the Protestant Reformation, the cultural development of New England and the formation of the Chilean Republic.

In this context, David Trumbull is seen as a catalytic agent of the creative tensions between the Roman Catholic and the Protestant ideologies and practices, and between the Latin American and the Anglo-Saxon ethos.

In relating the Gospel message to the needs and aspirations of the emerging nation-state, David Trumbull is considered as a precursor of the liberating forces which have made Chile one of the most stable and progressive republics in Latin America. His name is an *Open Sesame* for understanding the annals of this State, which in our times, seeks to create its own way of living.

It is hoped that the extrapolation of the insights, experiences and principles which these accultural processes narrate, may add a new dimension to the Christian World Mission in the fulfillment of its "Errand Into the Wilderness."

ACKNOWLEDGEMENTS

The author wishes to thank the following publishing agencies for permission to quote excerpts from copyright sources:

Alfred A. Knopf, Inc., *A History of Latin America*, by Hubert Herring, Second Edition Revised.
American Book Company, *The Puritans*, by Perry Miller and Thomas H. Johnson.
Charles Scribner's Sons, *A History of the Christian Church*, by Williston Walker, Revised Edition 1969.
Editorial del Pacifico, S.A., *El Protestantismo en Chile*, by Father Ignacio Vergara, S.J.
Fondo de Cultura Económica, *Las Ideas Políticas en Chile*, by Ricardo Donoso.
Harper & Brothers, *Yale and the Ministry*, by Roland H. Bainton.
Hutchinson Publishing Group LTD., *Heirs of Great Adventure: History of Balfour, Williamson & Company*, by Wallis Hunt.
Oxford University Press, *The History and Character of Calvinism*, by John T. McNeil.
Praeger Publishers, Inc., *Religion, Revolution and Reform*, by William V. D'Antonio and Frederick B. Pike.
University of North Carolina Press, *A History of Chile*, by Luís Galdames, Tr. by Isaac Joslin Cox, 1941.
University of Notre Dame Press, *Chile and United States Relations, 1880-1962*, by Frederick B. Pike.
Vanguard Press, Inc., *Puritanism and Democracy*, by Ralph Barton Perry.
Yale University Press, *Memorials of Eminent Yale Men*, by Anson Phelps Stokes; and *The Autobiography of Colonel John Trumbull*, ed. by Theodore Sizer.

The author wishes to thank the Yale University Library for permission to quote from a letter of David Trumbull to Edward Law Baldwin, of July 8, 1945. Also a letter to Theodore Dwight Woolsey of November 20, 1866.

In addition to the Yale University Library the author is indebted to the libraries of The American Bible Society, The Connecticut Historical Society, the Chilean National Library, and the library of the Hartford Seminary Foundation.

For biographical data concerning the Trumbull family, the writer is especially indebted to Miss Alice Trumbull, Mrs. Claire Trumbull Higgins, Mrs. Hester Trumbull Standish II, and Mrs. Elizabeth T. Barrett -- all granddaughters of David Trumbull; to Mrs. Jean Atwater Battin, great-granddaughter of David Trumbull, who edited the manuscript; and to William Trumbull, great-grandson of David Trumbull, who provided primary source materials for this narrative.

The writer is also indebted to colleagues who read the manuscript critically and made suggestions for its improvement, namely: Professor LeRoy Moore, Jr., Professor Edna M. Baxter, Professor J. Maurice Hohlfeld, and Professor James F. Hopewell.

For encouraging counsels, the writer wishes to acknowledge his indebtedness to his friends, Thomas S. Goslin II, Fred Field Goodsell, John H. Sinclair, and Ralph D. Winter.

Finally, the writer is indebted to Mrs. Ellen Pack, who as copy editor, improved the legibility and interpretation of the manuscript.

1

THE NEW ENGLAND HERITAGE

"Qui Transtulit Sustinet" (He Who Transplanted Sustains)

The life and works of David Trumbull (1819-1889) stands out in bold relief against the background of the Calvinistic-Puritan tradition which to a large measure fashioned the style of life in colonial New England. Calvinism in essence was an affirmation of God's intervention in the total affairs of men and the human response to the Divine initiative. However inadequate its interpretation was of the perennial paradoxes of good and evil, of determinism and freedom and of the relation of the sacred to the secular, it was a significant ideology of the Reformation Movement of the 16th century.

This Movement was inimical to the tyrannies of totalitarian forms of authority in church or state and envisioned the establishment of the City of Man upon the foundation of the City of God. The spirit of Calvinism is succinctly stated by John T. McNeill as follows:

> It is characterized by a combination of God-consciousness with an urgent sense of mission. The triune God, Sovereign Creator, Redeemer, and Comforter, is an ever-present reality through both prosperity and disaster. Guilt is real but it is submerged under grace.
>
> The Calvinist may not know how it happens; he may be a very simple minded theologian; but he is conscious that God commands his will and deed as well as his thought and prayer. This is what makes him a reformer and a dangerous character to encounter on moral and political issues. He is a man with a mission to bring to realization the will of God in human society.(1)

Calvinism as practiced by 17th century England gave rise to Puritanism, which in turn became a dominant factor in the 18th century New England culture and in the formation of the "American Mind." Perry Miller interprets the role of Puritanism as follows:

> Puritanism may perhaps best be described as that point of view, that philosophy of life, that code of values, which was carried to New England by the first settlers in the early seventeenth century. Beginning thus it has become one of the continuous factors in American life and American thought.
>
> Any inventory of the elements that have gone into the making of the "American Mind" would have to commence with Puritanism. . . Its role in American thought has been almost the dominant one, for the descendants of the Puritans have carried at least some habits of the Puritan mind into a variety of pursuits, have spread across the country, and in many fields of activity have played a leading part.
>
> The force of Puritanism, furthermore, has been accentuated because it was the first of these traditions to be fully articulated, and because it has inspired certain traits which have persisted long after the vanishing of the original creed. Without some understanding of Puritanism, it may be safely said, there is no understanding of America.(2)

Puritanism, confronting new social realities on the wilderness frontier, became the motif of what was called the "New England Theology." The Bible was interprated to provide the model of and for the individual and his society. Under the leadership of ministers who proclaimed the characteristically Puritan and Calvinistic Covenant Theology, a Congregational Commonwealth was established. The constitution of this body politic was called the "Fundamental Orders." Ralph Barton Perry gives a brief summary of these statutes:

> The Fundamental Orders of Connecticut, drafted in response to a sermon delivered by Thomas Hooker before the General Court of Hartford on May 31, 1638, has been referred to as "the first written constitution of modern democracy."
>
> The Biblical injunction, "Take ye wise men, and understanding, and known among your tribes, and I will make them rulers over you," was cited by Hooker with the emphasis on the *taking* rather than the *making*; and was interpreted as meaning "that the choice of public magistrates belongs to the people, by God's own allowance. They who have power to appoint officers and magistrates," he went on to say, "it is in their power also, to set the bounds and limitations of the power and place unto which they call them;" because in short, "the foundation of authority is laid, firstly, in the free consent of the people."(3)

The New England Heritage

The Congregational Commonwealth was bound to fail because it limited the franchise to a small minority who were supposed to be saints and tried to force the majority of sinners in the secular world to be Christian. It did, however, make significant gains in the experiments of community-living and by proclaiming the principle of voluntarism: that is, the non-fiscal and non-denominational administration and support of the activities of the church. After much travail of trial and error it disestablished the Church in 1818.(4) Article Seven of the Constitution of the State of Connecticut reads:

> It being the right of all men to worship the Supreme Being, the Great Creator and Preserver of the Universe and to render that worship in a mode consistent with the dictates of their consciences, no person shall by law be compelled to join or support, nor be classed or associated with, any congregation, church or religious association.
>
> No preference shall be given by law to any religious society or denomination in the state. Each shall have and enjoy the same and equal powers, rights and privileges and may support and maintain the ministers or teachers of its society or denomination, and may build and repair houses for public worship.(5)

This statute was in keeping with the First Amendment of the Constitution of the United States of America which was written in 1791 and stated, "Congress shall make no law respecting an established religion, or prohibiting the free exercise thereof."(6) The changes from persecution to religious tolerance of dissidents and the separation of Church and State were significant gains in the quest for the establishment of the ideal "Holy Commonwealth."

Another characteristic of the New England Heritage was the influence of what was called "The New Haven Theology." The core of Congregational ministers and professors of Yale College so interpreted the Calvinistic doctrines as to give rise to liberalism and evangelism. This trend was a preface to the *Second Great Awakening* which historian Williston Walker defines as follows:

> Beginning at the end of the eighteenth century, a mighty reawakening of religious interest swept the land. In New England, what was sometimes called the *Second Great Awakening* showed its first signs as early as 1792. By 1800, revival was in full tide. . . Conspicuous in leading the movement were the brilliant Yale president, Timothy Dwight (1752-1817), and the men he trained to carry on the work: Congregational preacher Lyman Beecher (1775-1863) and Yale theologian Nathaniel W. Taylor (1786-1858). . . A product of the awakening, destined to become the outstanding exponent of revivalism . . .was a young lawyer of upstate New York, Charles Grandison Finney (1792-1875).(7)

The evangelistic outreach of this "mighty reawakening" produced an ever-increasing number of benevolent and voluntary missionary societies. Young men of the colleges and seminaries of New England were stirred to offer themselves for missionary service at home and abroad. The renowned Haystack Prayer Meeting, inspired by the leadership of Samuel Mills (1783-1818) at Williams College in 1806 and similar student movements at Andover Theological Seminary gave rise in 1810 to the formation of the Board of Commissioners for Foreign Missions. The purpose of this Board was, "the salvation of men; the furtherance of the great purposes for which the Redeemer came down from heaven . . . to impart to those who sit in darkness and in the region and shadow of death, the saving knowledge of Christ."(8)

The American Bible Society was established in 1816. Article I of the Constitution reads "This Society shall be known as the American Bible Society of which the sole object shall be to encourage a wider circulation of the Holy Scriptures without note or comment."(9) The American Tract Society was instituted in 1825. Its object was "to diffuse a knowledge of our Lord Jesus Christ as the Redeemer of sinners and to promote the interests of vital godliness and sound morality, by the circulation of Religious Tracts, calculated to receive the approbation of all Evangelical Christians."(10) The American Seamen's Friend Society was established in 1826. Its purpose was "to preach the Gospel to seamen in every principal seaport in Popish, Mohammedan and Pagan Countries."(11) In 1839 the Foreign Evangelical Society was formed. Ten years later it was consolidated with the American Protestant Society and the Christian Alliance under the name of The American and Foreign Christian Union. Its purpose was ". . . by Missions, Colportage, the Press and other appropriate agencies, to diffuse and promote the principles of Religious Liberty and a pure and Evangelical Christianity, both at home and abroad, wherever a corrupted Christianity exists."(12) This Society was generously supported by the Protestant churches of New England. It would seem that the descendants of John Calvin (1509-1564), Oliver Cromwell (1599-1658), John Cotton (1584-1652), and Thomas Hooker (1586-1648), sincerely believed that they were people of God predestined to preach the Gospel to the entire world.

These five voluntary Missionary Societies shared the support of David Trumbull. Their apostle considered himself an agent of the Reformed Faith, called of God to preach the Gospel in the lands of the Golden Legend. It was, indeed, a daring adventure for him to fulfill such a mission in Latin America, where, in those days, the winds of intellectual, religious, industrial and political revolutions, which occurred in other parts of the Western world, were scarcely noticed.

In his student days at Yale College, at the age of twenty-six, David Trumbull wrote for the Hale Monument Association a play in five acts entitled "The Death of Captain Nathan Hale" in which he underscored the words, "I only regret that I have only one life to give for my country." No doubt the young author was inspired by the heroism of his fellow-countryman from Coventry, Connecticut for in that same year he chose to leave the comforts of home, church and nation in order to give himself in singular devotion to his fellowmen in a strange land who also were seeking the same rights to life and the pursuit of happiness proclaimed in the Constitution of the North American Commonwealth. Undaunted then, he went away fortified by the motto of his beloved state of Connecticut which is, "Qui transtulit sustinet." (He who transplanted sustains).

2
FAMILY PORTRAIT

Fortuna Favet Audaci (Fortune Favors the Brave)

In his autobiography, *Reminiscences and Letters*, John Trumbull (1756-1843) gave the following authentic information about the family genealogy:

> The families of Trumbull in New England have cause to believe themselves to be a branch of the Trumbulls of Scotland. In the year 1334 Robert Bruce, King of Scotland, on a hunting party, was attacked by a bull, and his life was in imminent danger from the animal, when a young peasant threw himself before the king, and with equal strength, dexterity and good fortune seized the bull by the horns, turned him aside, and thus saved the royal life. The king, grateful for the act, commanded the hitherto obscure youth to assume the name Trumbull,* gave him an estate near Peebles (which is still in the family), and a coat of arms -- three bulls' heads, with the motto, Fortuna Favet Audaci, still the bearings of the American branch.
>
> The first person of the name to be known on record in the United States is John Trumbull of Rowley, in the county of Essex, Massachusetts, who was made a free man in Boston in 1640. He is understood to have emigrated from Cumberland of Lancaster in England, on the borders of Scotland. A son of this person, named also John removed to Suffield in Connecticut; and one of his sons, Joseph, removed from Suffield to Lebanon. This was my grandfather, and was born at Suffield, 1679.

---

* Phonetical and regional pronunciations account for the variations in the spelling of the name Turnbull. It is written Trumble, Trimble, Trumbull, Trunsble, and several other ways.

Family Portrait

My father, Jonathan Trumbull was born at Lebanon in 1710. Joseph, his father, was a respectable, strong-minded, but uneducated farmer, who, feeling the disadvantages of his own want of education made it his first object to give to his children this first blessing of social life; and at an early age my father was placed at Harvard College, where he became a distinguished scholar, acquiring a sound knowledge of Hebrew as well as Greek and Latin languages, and all the other studies of that day. He was graduated with honors in 1727. He died in 1785, having been governor of the State of Connecticut, by annual election, during the entire war of the Revolution; and was the only person, who, being first magistrate of a colony in America before the separation from Great Britin, retained the confidence of his countrymen through the Revolution, and was annually re-elected governor to the end of that eventful period. My mother, Faith Robinson, daughter of John Robinson, minister of Duxbury in Massachusetts, was understood to be the great granddaughter of John Robinson, the father of the pilgrims, who led our Puritan ancestors (his parishioners) out of England in the reign of James V (sic),* and resided with them some years at Leyden in Holland, until in 1620 they emigrated to Plymouth in Massachusetts, and there, among other acts of wisdom and piety, laid foundations of that system of education in town schools, which has since been extended so widely over the northern and western parts of the United States, forming the glory and the defense, the *decus atque tutamen* of our country.(1)

James Hammond Trumbull (1821-1897) cousin and classmate of David Trumbull (1819-1889) wrote in his *Memorial History of Hartford County:*

Joseph, Sr. Trumbull, who moved to Suffield, Connecticut in 1670 and died in 1684 was the pioneer and founder of one of the most distinguished Connecticut families. Among his lineal descendants for generations are found governors, judges, legislators, ministers, historians, the poet and painter; not the least of these was his grandson, "Brother Jonathan," the war governor of the Revolution and the bosom friend of Washington.(2)

Not least of these distinguished descendants is the subject of our historical narration, David Trumbull, third generation removed from Governor Jonathan Trumbull, son of John Mason Trumbull and Hannah Wallace Tunis (1800-1823). David's father, John Mason Trumbull was born in Lebanon in 1774 and settled in Colchester, Connecticut in 1809.(3) After many adventures he made and spent several fortunes by way of export-import trade along the eastern seaboard and in plantation productions in Savannah, Georgia. He was married three times and had thirteen children in all. (4) His first wife was Anna H. Gibbons, daughter of the wealthy Thomas Gibbons who made his millions by establishing

---

* Should read James VI who ruled England and Scotland as James I, 1603-1625.

ferryboat routes from New Jersey to New York.(5) He settled in Elizabeth Town, New Jersey in 1814. Three articles written in the Elizabeth Daily Journal in July 1873 by a classmate of David Trumbull entitled "The Old Homes--Cherry Lawn" portray an illuminating account of the early home background of David Trumbull. The historic mansion was called "Cherry Lawn" because in the wide lot on the hill in the center of the town, former renowned citizens had planted a garden and an orchard in which were the attractive cherry trees. The Reverend William Hall, Yale College 1842 writes:

> It is as long ago as during our last war with England that Mr. John M. Trumbull from Connecticut succeeded his father-in-law, Thomas Gibbons, in occupying this property. We adverted in our last to the conspicuousness of the family in that State to which this gentleman belonged. This circumstance would naturally bring to Mr. Trumbull's pleasant New Jersey Home, society from its best circles. We learn from the same respected lady quoted in the last article, that the Wadsworths from Hartford were among their guests. The families were also related. The famous John Trumbull, first president of the American Society of Art and Design, his uncle, who was much in New York at that period, was no doubt often over here. . . The more modern part of this house, its tasteful and spacious northern half was added either by Mr. Trumbull or by his rich father-in-law. It was deeded by him to his grandson Gibbons Trumbull. This family while in Elizabeth, were regular attendants at the Presbyterian Church, under the then charge of that prince of pastors, the Rev. Dr. John McDowell. Mr. Trumbull became a member by certificate in 1815.
>
> We are indebted to the courtesy of James Hammond Trumbull, Esq., the learned President of the Connecticut Historical Society at Hartford, who so well sustains the credit of this ancient historic name of his native State, for the following particulars respecting this former well-known citizen of our town. John M. Trumbull, who married Anna, daughter of Thomas Gibbons, was a son of David Trumbull of Lebanon, Connecticut, third son of the first Governor Jonathan, and brother of the second Jonathan and of Colonel John the painter. Mr. John Mason Trumbull died in Colchester, Connecticut in 1859. He was thrice married and left children by each wife. His elder brother Joseph was the third Governor of the surname. He died in Hartford in 1861. Of the family of John's eldest son, Gibbons Trumbull, I know nothing. His second son, John Hayward, married a younger sister of Senator Lyman Trumbull who was a native of Colchester and a grandson of the Rev. Benjamin Trumbull who wrote the History of Connecticut.
>
> David, third son of John Mason Trumbull (by his second wife), was my classmate at Yale; went to South America in 1845 as a missionary of the American and Foreign Evangelical Union, built up a church at Valparaiso, Chile of which he became pastor about 1855, and has remained there with the exception of two or three short visits to the United States ever since. He has several

children of whom one of them is I believe, now at Yale. James
Hedden Trumbull, another son of John graduated at Yale 1848 and
is now Consul at Talcahuano, Chile. John's youngest daughter
Harriet, is the wife of Professor George J. Brush, of the Sheffield Scientific School, New Haven.

Mr. Trumbull's second wife was a Miss Tunis of Elizabeth of a
much respected family, and his third a Miss Eliza Bruen of Bellville, New Jersey, a lady of great worth, whose mother as I am
informed by my good friend and hers Mr. Abel C. Hatfield, was
originally from this town.

He also states that Gibbons Trumbull, who never married, died in
Illinois. Two married daughters of the first Mr. Trumbull are living in the city of New York. The Singer Sewing Maching Co's lots
at the Port were from the property of their father were devised
to these highly respectable ladies. But a few years ago, says Mr.
DeCasse, a clergyman who stated that he lived in South America,
called on him, to see once more, as he observed, his father's
house and his own birth place. It was the Rev. David Trumbull mentioned above. He called also at Mr. Mayo's on Jersey Street, with
his two sisters, and mentioned to his friends there as we learned
from one of them, that they had been to take a look at the old
home. How many pleasing, or, perhaps, trying souvenirs, mingled
as usual on memory's page must be interwoven, in the minds of such
visitors, with the objects and scents of dear familiar abodes of
early years! There some of life's sweetest flowers bloomed, and
others faded forever from the earthly sight. Our pen is not yet
done with Cherry Lawn. It has other family associations and names
on its record, to tempt and reward, if possible, an early aurevoir (Rev. William Hall).(6)

From such a distinguished biological ancestor and counting such a rich cultural heritage, David Trumbull was born
in the Cherry Lawn Mansion, of Elizabeth Town, New Jersey
to John Mason Trumbull and Hannah Wallace Tunis on November
1, 1819. He was the eldest of three children, Susan Landis
Trumbull died scarcely two months of age May 9, 1821, and
Julia Gorman Trumbull died at the age of seven in 1830. Unfortunately, David's mother also died at the age of 23 when
he was but four years of age.(7) Writing of his affection
for his loved ones and of his early sense of a calling he
wrote in his Journal of November of 1842:

I have had peculiar pious parents and have been peculiarly led in
life. . .and now I remain the sole representative -- and O may I
become a peculiar good and useful man!

Learning that my mother when dying prayed for and kissed her two
children and thinking that perhaps her spirit has known my course
in life -- I have wept at recalling many a sin and thought how was
it possible to do so-against what life, what prayers, teachings,
motives, knowledge and against what Divine Love has my life of sin

been pursued! Why spared when others less wicked have been cut off -- others allowed their own way of sin -- but what mercy has followed me as it were, out from the fire! O my Master, bring in others also, my family, my classmates all my acquaintances, and aid me with Thy strength to mend the breach I have made by a life of holiness and activity.(8)

Without doubt, David Trumbull was brought up in a Christian home and early in life was exposed to the teachings of the church. When his mother died, David was brought up by his maternal grandmother, Patience Meeker Camp (1759-1831) -- a woman of strong religious convictions and refinement. (9) The name of his father, John Mason Trumbull, appears on the role of the Presbyterian Church of Elizabethtown, New Jersey, having been received by transfer of letter in 1815. In the same record information is given about the minister of the church and the Sunday School;

> In 1804 the Rev. John McDowell was the ordained pastor of this church. Under his preaching large accessions were made to the church. On August 27, 1814, the first Sunday School was established in Elizabethtown largely through his efforts and notwithstanding the opposition of those who were not convinced that it was a worthy institution. He was moderator of the General Assembly in 1820.(10)

Having been subject to the allurements and adventures of those relatives who made their fortunes as trader-merchants, it was natural that young David would be expected to pursue the same profession. And so it was that "in his thirteenth year he served as a clerk in a retail dry-goods store in Newark, New Jersey and afterwards in a wholesale dry-goods establishment in New York City. But his determination to become a merchant was suddenly and finally arrested by the Great Panic of 1836-1837 in which the New York House S. and T. Door and Company, with which he was connected, failed. It was this incident that brought him to college. His family, having removed to Colchester, Connecticut, David returned to his home in 1837 and at once entered upon a course of classical studies in Bacon Academy in that place under the able tuition of Myron N. Morris (Yale College 1837) and Edward Strong (Yale College 1838) both of whom strongly urged him to prepare for college, which he did, entering our class as a sophomore in 1839."(11) Many years later David Trumbull "often recurred with pleasantry this experience in commercial life."(12)

After graduating from Yale College, New Haven, in 1842, David Trumbull was offered a scholarship to study for the ministry at Princeton Theological Seminary in New Jersey. The scholarship was offered "by the kindly, venerable and reverend friend, D. F. Backus Esq., of Philadelphia."(13)

Family Portrait

The Rev. William E. Dodge, son-in-law and co-pastor of David Trumbull gave the following information for this period of David's life:

> At the close of the course of three years, he was ordained as an Evangelist, and in response to a plea presented by the Foreign Evangelical Society in behalf of this West Coast, accepted an appointment to come to Valparaiso to preach, first to seafaring men, and to prepare the way for Christian work on shore in English and Spanish as rapidly as possible.
>
> Referring to this step in his private journal, he wrote in March 1845, "It seems as though a field is opened there, and in some respects as though I am fitted to enter and till it, and scattering seed, to wait patiently for God to give the increase."(14)

In another chapter the story will be told of the education of David Trumbull at Yale College and at Princeton Theological Seminary and his call to be an agent of the Reformed faith on the Southern Continent. Our present concern is with the family portrait.

In this portrait there stands out with impressive distinction the one who was destined to be the helpmate of David Trumbull for thirty-nine years. No doubt David Trumbull met Jane Wales Fitch during his student days at Yale College 1839-1842. The consummation of this encounter by their marriage at Smithfield, North Carolina, on June 5th, 1850 was the purpose of David's return to his native land in December 1849.

Like the Trumbulls the Fitch families also traced their descendants from the British Isles and by way of Puritan forbears. Among them they counted a long line of ministers, military, magistrates and teachers. Jane's father was Allan Fitch (1785-1839) a descendant of governor James Fitch (1649-1721), a clock-maker who with his wife Harriet West Morning (1802-1874) were proprietors of a plantation in North Carolina. The fortunes of her parents were lost due to the tragedies of the Civil War. The army of General Sherman camped on their grounds bringing much destruction. (15) Allan Fitch, who administered the plantation died when his daughter Jane was fifteen years of age. She was taken under the care of her uncle, the Rev. Eleazar T. Fitch who was professor Homilectics at the Divinity School of Yale College from 1817 to 1852.(16)

Living in New Haven, Connecticut, during these early years Jane Fitch belonged to the Yale College Faculty family. Names of renowned professors and ministers were household names to her. Amongst them were such men as the Rev. Nathaniel W. Taylor, Dr. Noah Porter, Professor

Benjamin Silliman, the Rev. Lyman Beecher and the Rev. Leonard Bacon.

The story is told about the abortive love affair between Delia Bacon, sister of the Rev. Leonard Bacon, pastor of Center Church in New Haven, and a young divinity student, Alexander McWhorter. The discrepancy in age between the two gave rise to critical comments and a six-year feud between the Bacon and the Taylor families resulted. The affair ultimately brought about adverse relations between the Divinity School Faculty and the Parochial Clergy. "All might have been avoided," wrote Professor Roland Bainton, had intimate friends been gifted with the graces of silence, but Miss Jane Fitch, the niece of Professor Eleazar T. Fitch, reported that McWhorter had permitted some of Delia's letters to be read by others."(17) However much to be censured was the indiscretion of the young Jane Wales Fitch, that of her elderly monitors was much more so. Professor Bainton closed his comments on this bizarre episode with these words:

> What a spectacle of a company of able, idealistic, courageous and usually sensible people rent for six years over a brief infatuation! Strange that this community which lacked the capacity to deal with itself did have real wisdom in dealing with the nation.(18)

The Puritan New England heritage is vividly portrayed even in the response of Jane Wales Fitch to the courtship-by-mail from Valparaiso, Chile, on the part of David Trumbull. All considerations and commitments were made by both parties out of a sense of duty and for the glory of God. In her private journal of October 5, 1948, from New Haven, Jane wrote:

> Today I am anxiously asking myself can I consent to take Mr. Trumbull for my companion through life. He is a devoted minister of Christ and for this I love him. He was, when last I saw him agreeable as a friend -- but can I love him sufficiently to take upon me the responsibility of a wife? O for light and guidance from above! I am surprised that I do not say "no" without any questioning, but something within me forbids this. I have asked very frequently of late in prayers that God would make me useful in His vineyard and now there seems to be an answer from Him. This causes me to stop ere I decide, and yet if I should consent to try in God's help to fulfill these duties, and should find my feelings changed toward Mr. T. when I see him what should I do? I should then give him reason to hope and would bring sorrow or discomfort to us both. . . .If I could only see Mr. T. then I could judge how far I might trust myself to act -- but he too is taking a great risk -- He has not seen me in years -- three or more, and how does he know that I shall please him when we meet?

I hope my character has improved but then it has greatly changed.
Oh if he had only waited till he came home before he had made his
proposition. I should be glad--but if it is done and I am to decide
the great question--now that I have as I trust decided the only
greater of my life--I have laid subject before my Heavenly Father
and I can now only wait to see how my heart inclines. I have been
to see a sabbath scholar--Emily White--this afternoon and talked
with her about her soul's salvation. I hope with trembling that she
is a child of God.(19) . . .Auntie Dana was at Be Mc.'s last evening and she talked much with me about Mr. T. I suspect he loved
her but know that he never offered himself--Well I hope I may be
allowed to make his life very happy. I feel sure that my religious
character will grow under his influence and I hope he will not suffer from me. I never felt more need, more desire for holiness of
heart and life since I accepted his proposal. I seems to me that I
have now taken almost the last step in my earthly existence before
the one that will be the last when I shall make my exit from this
world of sin--one I trust of perfect happiness. . .

This afternoon I went with Eliza to call on Mary Merwin and then
alone to see Mary Blake. While I was there Dr. Leonard Bacon came
in--I have not met him before since the trial (of Alexander Mc-
Whorter) there was an "awful pause" for a few seconds, but soon
the stiffness wore off and when all were conversing pleasantly I
took my leave.

My sabbath scholars were all present Sunday Morning--all had a
lesson well learned. Oh that they might give evidence of piety
while I am with them!

In her *Journal* of July 25, 1850, Jane wrote:

Husband has gone to New York to engage our stateroom on the Crescent City. Everyone seems to be sad to have us take this route
(by way of crossing the Isthmus at Panama) at this season, but I
have no fears. Our duty seems to be to go this way. It is ours
to do that and to leave the consequences with our God.

August 2nd 1850 - Yesterday we bade goodbye to our native land and
commenced our journey to Valparaiso. . .Messrs. Spaulding and Brigham came to say goodbye. Mr. Brigham gave me a Spanish Testament. . .

Monday August 5, 1850 - I have entirely recovered from seasickness
and am enjoying our voyage very much--delightful weather. The sun-
sets and the nights are glorious. On Saturday evening David and I
watched the grotesque clouds that bordered the horizon near sunset
and made all manners of figures. We looked till daylight faded away
with darkness and the stars came out one by one till the heavens
were crowded with them. Now fully our hearts respond to the words
of the Psalmist, "The heavens declare Thy glory." We return to our
room at nine o'clock.

Yesterday A.M. husband preached at the request of the captain. His
text was "The fear of the Lord is clean and enduring forever."
His sermon was very good and listened to with attention. It was

a serious solemn service to me out on the vast deep worshipping our Creator whose power over one is realized here more than anywhere else. . . I enjoyed the Sabbath very much--read my Bible and the life of Rev. John Newton. His long career of wickedness makes me have some hope for my poor brother--God's power is mighty to save. Oh that I had more faith for my brother and that I should pray with more conviction!

As these daring Yankee conquistadors journeyed to the lands of the Golden Legand, they recorded for history their impressions of frontier villages and conditions of peoples who were desperately in need of the mercy and grace of God. Brief notes in Jane's Journals read like exciting adventures of the sixteenth century conquistadors in search for a different kind of gold. Upon the arrival at Port Royal, Jamaica August 8, 1850, Jane Fitch Trumbull wrote in her Journal:

Coffee is black gold. I was not very favorably impressed with the people of Jamaica as represented by the people we had on board or by those dreadful filthy people who came on board for them.

August 10 - The land of South America is in sight. What cause we have for gratitude that our voyage has been as prosperous and pleasant as possible! I became quite well acquainted with Dr. Lique's wife. We are the only ladies on board since the passengers left us at Port Royal.

August 12, 1850 - Chagres River. David goes ashore to make some arrangement for the trip by land and to seek accommodations in the miserable filthy town of Chagres. Problem of staying on board ship or going to the wicked place on Sunday. Chagres belongs to the New Granada--the fortifications are three hundred years old--the first ruins I have ever seen. Stop at Gatun Village--sleep on board instead of going ashore to sleep in the rancho of the natives. How sad that one should come from a civilized christian land to brutalize these poor ignorant people. The vegetation is luxurious. The birds make a great noise--turkey buzzards, cocoa palms and a hundred other trees.

August 14, 1850 - Las Cruces. Oh what cause for thankfulness. Here we are safe at Cruces, the dangers are passed!

Now the journey must be taken across a stretch of twenty miles over the lands which in the twentieth century were to become the location of the Panama Canal. Jane wore trousers for the tedious horseback ride across the jungle stretch. Brief notes recorded her reactions to the "superstitions of drunken and cursing pagans." She told of rats and plagues of cholera and rough terrain but interspersed with descriptions of human degradation Jane was moved to say "Oh what cause for thankfulness! What shall I render to the Lord for all His benefits to me?"(20)

Family Portrait 15

The story is told by her granddaughter of the trip down the West Coast of Chile. Jane Trumbull wept because she could hardly endure the onslaught of fleas. But then she explained to David "I weep not so much for the affliction of the fleas but more because I am making life more miserable for you by my weeping."(21)

Such is the image of the damsel from New England who was called of God to be the life-long companion of David Trumbull. Her ardent prayers were graciously answered by the Sovereign Lord whom she adored. In spite of the "risk" she did become "useful in His vineyard" and she did love him sufficiently to "take upon herself the responsibilities of a wife."

As the young couple started their ministry in Valparaiso, Chile, Mrs. Trumbull helped finance the enterprise by teaching in a School for Ladies and by taking in boarders from the foreign-speaking colony. Through the vicissitudes of the long years of voluntary exile from New England Holy Commonwealth she was a tower of strength to the missionary statesman-in-the making. After all she was the mother of nine children who made up the family portrait and whom we shall proceed to identify. Jonathan was the first child born in Valparaiso, Chile in 1851. In the genealogical records of the Trumbull family, the names of David and Jonathan appear so often that it would seem that it meant to honor the Biblical allusion of brotherly love. It is worthy of note that many given names of New England inhabitants and names of their towns were taken from the Scriptures -- as though new actors and new places were involved in the enactment of salvation history. New England was to become New Canaan and from Lebanon, Connecticut pioneers would go to the far south to establish new frontiers of the Kingdom branching out from Valparaiso, Chile.

The second progeny was called "Allan" -- no doubt to honor the heritage of the Fitch family. It was indeed a severe test for these young servants of the Lord when these first two descendants died while still very young.

David Trumbull Jr. was born at Valparaiso, Chile on May 31, 1855. He was the apple of his father's eye. Now surely his father must have thought that the long line of splendor of ministerial service would be assured. What an ideal relationship existed between the father and the son and what a lovely home the family shared together! David's younger brother John described this home and life together, writing:

> With all that my father did, he ever found time to be with and to help his children. After my father married Jane Wales Fitch,

niece of Eleazar T. Fitch, professor of Divinity at Yale, in 1850, they came to Chile on an independent basis, supporting themselves by conducting a young ladies' school for eight or ten years; when at the request of Union Church, he consented to give it up and devote himself entirely to pastoral and church work, though they were only able to offer as a salary half of what he was then making.

At that time I can remember that we had to give up horse-back riding--for my brother David and I had been in the habit of riding out to Fisherman's Bay every morning with father for a dip and a swim --in fact I was but five when he taught us to swim, and even to jump off the spring board into deep water--and take to footing it. He believed in all manly sports, which accoridng to him, included everything but shooting of which he never approved; and taught us or encouraged us to walk, run, play cricket, ride, climb, swim, dive, row, fish, cook, and so forth. On holidays we often went off on picnics to the country as a family, or up the hills and ravines back of Valparaiso, and were taught like the Boy Scouts of the present day, to be self-reliant and ready for any emergency.(22)

What a lovely home! What a lively hope! And with what sacrifice was David Trumbull Jr. sent off to Yale College to prepare for the high calling! But then what disappointment and trial-by-fire were still to temper the souls of David and Jane Trumbull! The biographical record of Yale College, Class of 1878, reads as follows:

David Trumbull, son of Rev. David Trumbull, Yale '42 and Jane W. (Fitch) Trumbull, was born May 31, 1855, at Valparaiso, Chile, where his father spent the greater part of his life as a Missionary. His son was sent to the United States to be educated, and was one of the original members of our Class. After graduation he spent a year at Valparaiso, and in 1877 returned to New Haven and entered the Yale Divinity School.

He was a member of the University Crew during that year and in the annual boat race with Harvard at New London, June 28, 1878, rowed No. 7 on the Yale Crew.

Five days later he lost his life in the brave and successful attempt to save the life of another from drowning. A small son of Col. Charles M. Coit of New London fell overboard from his father's yacht. Both Trumbull and Col. Coit leaped in to the water. The yacht was brought about successfully, and the boy was saved unharmed, but both his rescuers had sunk. Trumbull's body was not found until a week later, on June 10, 1878, when it was washed ashore near the scene of his heroic death. He was buried in New Haven the next day. From his youth up he had been a strong and fearless swimmer. John B. Kendrick of our Class, who was its secretary at that time, summed it up most acceptably: "The impulse of self-sacrifice which closed his life was thoroughly in keeping with the noble purposes which controlled it."(23)

Family Portrait

Such a terrible event would naturally be enough to embitter any human being but the man of God, as Job of Old would say, "though He slay me, yet will I trust Him" and so we read in the Journal of the Rev. David Trumbull for August 17, 1878:

> O dreadful blow!--it has touched me keenly! Then follows the prayer:
>
> O, may it correct and sanctify me--to perfect my thoughts and to brush out evil imaginations--to be more faithful in dealing with young persons in my flock! O that it may lead all my sons to enter into the ministry! God knows whom to gather in transcendant wisdom: precious in His sight is the death of his saints.

The Sovereign Lord was not unmindful to the ardent and frequent petitions of His servant David. His sons did go into the ministry but in ever-wider a field. John Trumbull (1856-1920) ministered to body, mind, and soul of peoples of local, national, and international communities. It is truly amazing how John Trumbull embodied the skills of science, art, philosophy and religion in this wider ministry: In the Quarter-Centenary Record--Yale '78, Biographical Sketches we read:

> Born at Valparaiso, Chile, September 28, 1856, and prepared for college at Mackay's School at Valparaiso and at the Stamford Military Institute of Stamford, Connecticut. . .College honors, etc. Delta Kappa, Psi Upsilon, and Linonia. Played on our Football twenty in Freshman and Sophomore years. Rowed on the losing crew in a race between two crews from our Class in Senior year. Taught at Bethany Mission. At Junior Exhibition he received a Second Dispute, as he did at Commencement when he was one of the speakers.
>
> *Later Career* - He spent the first year after graduation in graduate studies at the Sheffield Scientific School, and then he studied medicine at the Harvard Medical School where he received the degree of M.D. in 1883. For eighteen months he was house surgeon at the Boston City Hospital. He then went to Europe, and spent six months in studying in Vienna, after which he returned to Valparaiso, where he received, in 1884 the degree of Physician and Surgeon at the University of Chile. In September, 1894, he went with his family to "the States" spending a year at Montecito, in Southern California, and then returned to Valparaiso and took up his profession again, in which he has been very successful. He published in the Medical Record of New York, of August 21, 1897 a "Case of Eustrongylus Gigas," one of the rarities of medical literature, and in 1892, a pamphlet, A Challenge: Chile's Vindication and wrote an article for the Nation (New York) on the Chilean Revolution, 1891-1892. He has contributed on Medical topics to the *New York Medical Record* and the *Boston Medical and Surgical Journal*. . .

He attends the Union Church which was first gathered up by his father and organized into a church in 1847. He is a member of the governing body of the Union Church corporation. He is a director of the Valparaiso Bible Society, and of the Sheltering Home and Orphanage maintained by public charity in behalf of children of foreign parentage, who are left in want or destitution.

The name of John Trumbull entered the annal of international political history when he stoutly defended his beloved second fatherland in the above mentioned pamphlet *A Challenge: Chile's Vindication*. His brief report speaks volums:

> The conscientious dignified arraignment of U. S. officials for deceitful practices, speculative intrigues, and meddlesome espionage, during our revolution in 1891, though accompanied by incontestable documentary proof of what was claimed, only drew forth unworthy flings against a certain *Señor Jean Trumbull*. It is to me a genuine source of satisfaction, to recall the part I bore in trying to put the *Baltimore incident* in its true light, unmasking the unworthy practices of men whose political services were paid for by appointments to consular and diplomatic posts, for which they were unfit, and therefore unworthy to represent your country and her interests. The sooner you realize that successful wirepulling is to be paid for in some other way than at the expense of your national honor and advantage, the better. The pernicious spoils system makes us often heartily ashamed of the men who come out as representative Americans. Will not the '78 men aim to uproot this evil, and place consular and diplomatic services on a different footing?(24)

Dr. John Trumbull M.D., beloved physician of Valparaiso, added to the *mystique* that made the family name an *Open Sesame* in the annals of Chilean history. He so identified himself with Chile that he dedicated his creative gifts to paeans in poetic rhythm in his volume *Adean Melodies*. This inspired collection of 114 poems is dedicated to "Alice" his daughter to whom the writer is indebted for the privilege of reading the Journals of her grandparents.

In *Adean Melodies* the author speaks to the depths and aspirations of the soul. The divine design is apprehended by way of common place experiences in human life and the mystic messages in nature.

Thus we read of *A Child's Lullaby, My Whistling Boy; La Siempreviva* (the dainty blue-and-white everlasting flower which cover the barren Chilean hills); of the ever-present Chilean sparrow he writes:

> Perched on the spire of yonder tree
> A *diuca*, with fine gallantry,

Family Portrait 19

> Poured forth his heart's glad ecstasy
> In few, yet mellow, liquid notes.

He sings of valleys and rivers and surging sea; the tinges of beauty of sunrise and sunset on the towering mountains -- In healing tones he touches the imponderables of pain, suffering, death and immortality. Perhaps with the loss of David Jr. he wrote:

Makers of History

> The witless world gives him who plants the flag
> And roots it on the stubborn, shell plowed hill,
> Booming acclaims of noisy victory;
> When often he who, clambering up that crag,
> Met death half-way, and at its foot sleeps still
> Fired the shot which altered history.(25)

Stephen Trumbull was born in Valparaiso, Chile, February 15, 1858. In 1873 he was sent to New Haven, Connecticut to prepare for Yale College. He finished his preparatory studies at the Hopkins Grammar School in 1874. He graduated from Yale College in 1880. In the fall of 1880 he entered Harvard Medical School until 1882 when he was called back to Chile due to his father's heart attack. He spent ten months at the Royal Naval Hospital. He returned to the Harvard Medical School and received his medical degree in 1884. From 1884 to 1886 he served as resident physician in the Rhode Island General Hospital at Providence.

In the Journal of Prayer Notes of Stephen's father for June 9, 1880 we read:

> This morning have asked that Stephen may be guided and led to seek the ministry. On August 12 of the same year the note reads: Pray of late that Stephen may be roused to serve Christ and be led to preach Him, seems not inclined.

In History of the Class of 1880, Yale College Biographies the record is continued:

> . . . after the service in Rhode Island General Hospital started back to Chile where he intended to practice in Valparaiso. There was some delay in crossing the Isthmus of Panama and he took advantage of a few hours of leisure to visit a hospital for the purpose of studying yellow fever. During his visit he became infected with the disease and died at sea, June 7, 1886 (off Payta). In one of his letters relating his journeys between Chile and America he referred to "the marvelous amount of work performed by DeLesseps in ten months" . . . it is interesting to note that under the American Administration, yellow fever has been entirely eradicated from the canal zone. . . "Steve" was

a man of unusual force of character and of great ability, and possessed certain traits which called forth the affection and respect of his classmates to an exceptional degree.(26)

Again, David Trumbull's prayers were answered -- but in a different way. The conquest of disease is just as important as the conquest of sin.

Mary Trumbull was born at Valparaiso, Chile December 2, 1859. She was sent to Wellesley College, Massachusetts for her education. Her father, in the *Record*, described the College thus: "This college for ladies is situated 16 miles from Boston on a beautiful lake called Waban Mere. It was founded by Henry Durant, Esq. whose aim was to promote female education dedicated to our Lord Jesus Christ. In accordance with the founder of the College the first sermon of each college year is from the text, 'God is Love.'"

The prayer in David Trumbull's Journal for December 2, 1878 reads:

> That Mary, whose birthday was today, may be spared and directed in life to useful works and that money be provided for her education.(27)

But alas this promising young girl, died suddenly at Valparaiso, Chile in May of 1882. She suffered a heart attack while out riding with Mr. A. M. Merwin, a colleague of her father's.

Years later, a son-in-law and associate pastor of David Trumbull recorded this tribute to the long-suffering, steadfast-in-the-faith parents:

> Mrs. Trumbull stood by his side in sorrow and in joy, sharing his toil unto the end. Let her noble part be remembered!... for much that he did was through her daily help and supporting love. The trials they passed through when some of their young children were taken, and in later years when their beloved David and Mary and Stephen were called away in the flower of manhood and of womanhood, and all so unexpectedly, would seem to many to be too heavy to be borne; but God gave strength to his chosen ones who, with living faith continued to look into Immanuel's land knowing that they would see their dear ones.(28)

William Trumbull was born at Valparaiso, Chile December 25, 1861. As a young man he was very active in the community. He was in charge of the *Escuela Popular* and a leader in the Young Men's Institute. He too was urged to enter the ministry. In the Record we read:

Mr. William Trumbull and Mr. G. E. Tupper embarked on the 4th
of January, (1877) in the German steamship *Memphis* for Havre,
Liverpool and New York. Mr. William purposes to join the Theological department of Yale College. A letter from Yale College
October 2, 1887 gives a full account of the lectures of Professor
Henry Drummond who was sent by the students of the University of
Edinburgh on an evangelistic tour to the Universities and Colleges
of the United States.

Young William stressed the point that here was a *layman*
who was preaching the Gospel message in a way that captured the minds and lives of the best of the students.(29)
Lay witness to the faith was to characterize the life of
William Trumbull. He specialized in Journalism and Law.
His record reads as follows:

> Trumbull taught in Valparaiso 1883-1886 and was in business
> there 1887. He then studied at the Yale Law School (LL.B *magna
> cum laude* 1889) and practiced law in New Haven till 1896, being
> librarian of the Yale Law School 1895-1896 . . . he spends much
> time in travel and has been abroad continuously since 1907. He
> has published *The Problem of Cain*; A Study in the Treatment of
> Criminals; A Book of Poems (The Legend of the White Canoe) and
> *The Priestess of Humanity, Uncle Sam's Dilemma* and *Evolution and
> Religion:* A Parents Talks with His Children on the Moral side
> of Evolution.(30)

William Trumbull was married March 30, 1891 to Anne
Leavenworth Train and settled in Litchfield, Connecticut.
We find him very active as a layman in the local church.
Six children constitute the biological link and media by
which the New England Heritage still prevails.

The lay witness of the Trumbull descendants is also
recorded in the annals of the Chilean Republic. James
Hedden Trumbull, second child of John Mason Trumbull and
his third wife Eliza Bruen was born at Elizabeth, New
Jersey January 16, 1828. He graduated at Yale College
the year 1848 and then received his Medical degree from
the College of Physicians and Surgeons in New York City.
He settled in Talcahuano, Chile and practiced medicine
for many years. He was the first North American physician
to pass the medical examinations and to receive the Chilean M.D. degree. In 1872 he was made a member of the
National Academy of Sciences. His son Richard, nephew of
David, also had a brief but distinguished participation in
the life of the Chilean Republic. His Biographical Sketch
reads as follows:

> Richard Lindsay Trumbull, the eldest child of Dr. James H.
> Trumbull (Yale College 1848) and Eulojia (Lindsay) Trumbull, was
> born in Talcahuano, Chile, on March 19, 1860. He received his
> early education in Valparaiso and was subsequently sent to New
> England to prepare for the Scientific School.

After graduation he studied for two years in the Yale Law School, interrupting his work in the meantime to act as attache to the Chilean Legation in Washington. He was graduated as LL.B. in 1883 and then followed another years' study of law in Europe, and to this was superadded, after his return to Chile, two years further study in the University of Santiago.

As a practicioner of law in Santiago he was mainly occupied as counsel for the large North American corporations doing business in that Country, such as the Telephone, Electric Light and Palace Car companies. He acted also as counsel for the United States Legation, in extradition of American criminals.

He early entered politics, and affiliated with the Radical wing of the Chilean Liberal Party. During the struggle of the Congressionalists against President Balmaceda in 1891, he became to the United States as a special agent of the revolutionists, and while thus engaged was also a supplementary delegate to the Lower House in the Chilean National Congress, in which he had already sat in 1887, and to which he was again elected deputy after his return home from his mission.

The brilliant ability with which he advocated the cause of his country in this period won him new distinction and has added a deeper pang to his early loss. He died suddenly from an attack of brain fever while spending a vacation at his father's home in Talcahuano, on February 1, 1894, aged nearly 34 years.(31)

Anita Trumbull was born in Valparaiso June 29, 1863. Her daughter, Claire T. Van Lennep (Mrs. Charles H. Higgins) provided the writer with much of the genealogical data for this family portrait. Julia Trumbull was the last of the nine children of the David Trumbull-Jane Wales Fitch family. She was born in Valparaiso July 25, 1865- She married the Rev. William Edwin Dodge of Ionia, Michigan, associate and successor minister of David Trumbull of Union Church in Valparaiso. Her daughter, Anita Trumbull Dodge (Mrs. Anita Huntington Atwater) portrays her mother as follows:

> Julie Trumbull was a little goddess of Spring. Her voice was miniature and melodiously sweet. Her eyes were as violet-blue as the Chilean sky -- her hair sprinkled with gold dust -- her mind conjured up everything rare and charming. She was born to stay rare and charming.(32)

The following story adds luster to the entire family portrait -- Anita Trumbull and her sister Julia were students at Wellesley College in 1886. While on a vacation trip on Nantucket Island, Massachusetts, they were surprised to notice the name of their native city painted on the door of a cottage. With trepidation they inquired of the owner -- a retired sailor, why he painted the word

"Valparaiso" on his door? "Because," he said "David Trumbull and his lady-angel Missus brought me back to health when I was dying with black smallpox -- then sent me back to New Bedford -- they changed the whole course of my life. Young ladies, all my life till I swallowed the anchor, roughly speaking, -- that's why Valparaiso is painted on my door. My home, after travellin' round the world fifty times to find it. That town is just like it sounds -- a Valley of Paradise."(33)

In presenting the Trumbull family portrait mention was made of the sons and close relatives of David Trumbull who were educated at Yale College, New Haven. How fitting then that on the gateway of their Alma Mater there appears the Trumbull coat-of-arms of the three bulls and the motto, "Fortuna favet Audaci" (Fortune favors the Brave).

REV. DAVID TRUMBULL D.D.

JANE WALES FITCH TRUMBULL

DAVID TRUMBULL

DAVID TRUMBULL

JANE WALES FITCH TRUMBULL

STEPHEN TRUMBULL

DAVID TRUMBULL JR.

THOMAS TRUMBULL GIBBONS

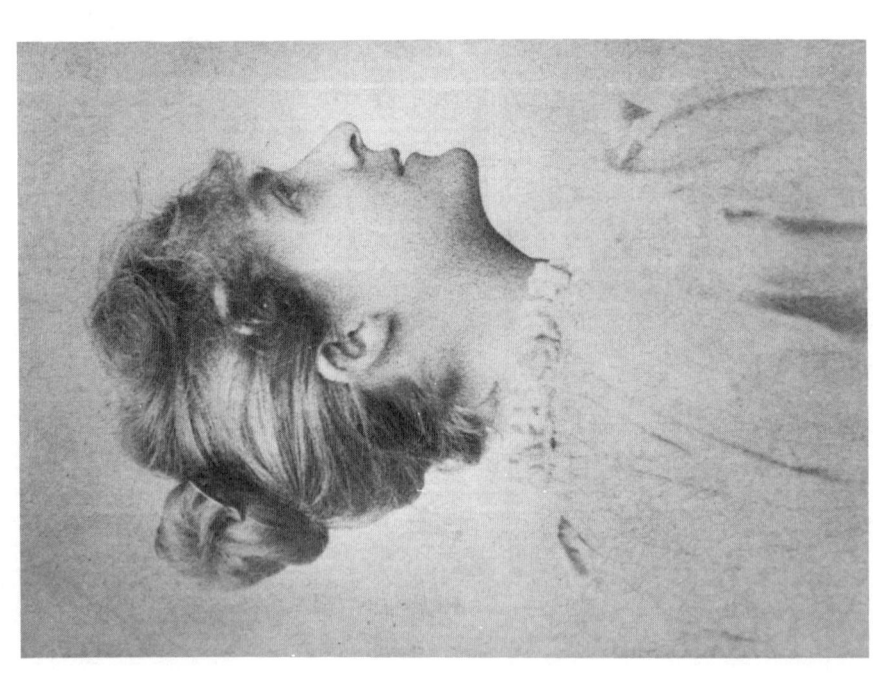

MARY TRUMBULL

WILLIAM TRUMBULL

JOHN TRUMBULL M.D. AND FAMILY

WILLIAM E. DODGE

JOHN TRUMBULL M.D.

ANITA TRUMBULL

JULIA TRUMBULL

3
EDUCATION AND CALL TO SERVICE

"Errand in the Wilderness"

In his book *Yale and the Ministry* Roland Bainton writes:

> The founding fathers of Yale were committed to 'the grand errand' of propagating 'the blessed Reformed Protestant religion in this wilderness' whereunto they deemed the religious education of suitable youth a chief expedient. . . The marrow of their hope was derived from John Calvin, who believed that the sovereign Lord had a plan for the ages to be achieved through his chosen people.(1)

Anson Phelps Stokes in his *Memorials of Eminent Yale Men* concurs with the above quotation:

> The college was founded by certain ministers 'for upholding and propagating the Christian Protestant Religion -- and that Christianity has continued the faith of their successors'. . . The New England Theology -- the most distinctive of American Theological Movements is almost exclusively a Yale produce.(2)

By way of David Trumbull's Journal and correspondence with alumni secretaries we can trace the steps toward Yale College and Princeton Theological Seminary, and note how faithfully his education and call to service, in keeping with the purposes and ideologies of the schools and churches of his day, were the formative factors in his life.

To the Alumni Secretary of Princeton Seminary David wrote on January 3, 1878:(3)

> I may add that in youth I never dreamed of being a minister--I set our to be a merchant and followed business for five years until

32

Providence, answering my deceased mother's and grandmother's prayers, led me back to school and college, and then as distinctly as ever I was led in anything, to Princeton Seminary to prepare for the ministry and then hither to try to do it here.

Myron N. Morris and Edward Strong, Yale graduates and David Trumbull's teachers at Bacon Academy, Colchester, Connecticut, had no difficulty in persuading their pupil to continue his studies at Yale. So well had they fulfilled their mission, that David entered Yale College as a sophomore in 1839.

The Trumbull family was closely related to the College for many years. Governor Jonathan Trumbull, the elder, was a member of the Corporation of the School as long as he was in office. Miss Harriet Trumbull (1783-1850), daughter of the second Governor Trumbull, married Professor Benjamin Silliman (1779-1864), distinguished professor of chemistry and natural sciences.(4) Professor Eleazar T. Fitch, professor of homiletics in the Divinity School (1822-1852), was David's uncle-in-law. President Theodore Dwight Woolsey (1801-1889), who served from 1846-1871, was David's teacher. The Reverend Leonard Bacon (1803-1881), pastor of Center Church, New Haven, was counselor to Jane Wales Fitch and David Trumbull. This close relationship is noted in David Trumbull's Class Letter in 1888:(5)

> How antique the men of 1792 did look, when you and I graduated! Even younger men then seemed old. My first entrance in Yale life was in 1839, at the Phi Beta Kappa oration, when Professor Silliman, the elder -- 'Uncle Ben' took me in with him -- past Chancellor Kent, Dr. Robinson (Edward) -- Professors Goodrich, Woolsey, Olmstead, and other grey-haired sires, through the middle aisle of Center Church, to the very front seat, and there seated me by his side to hear Dr. Leonard Bacon deliver a lecture, or oration rather, on the characteristics of American literature. Such a boy among such patriarchs, who knew more in one day than ever I had known in all my life! I wonder whether we look as old now to any young people as they did then to us! Well, good-bye. Send me the annual letter and the quinquennial report, and here are $5 to help pay the printer.(6)

John Mason Trumbull, David's father, was a student in Yale College but did not graduate. David's sister Harriet married Professor George J. Brush, director of Yale's Sheffield Scientific School. James Hammon Trumbull (1821-1897), David's cousin and classmate, was an encyclopedic scholar, philologist, member of the National Academy of Science and President of the Connecticut Historical Society from 1863-1889, and the Watkinson Library, Hartford from 1863-1893.

In those days Yale College also was astir due to the Second Great Awakening during which the revivalist Charles G. Finney took so prominent a part. These trends are clearly reflected in the Journals of David Trumbull. One notes an agony of spirit as David Trumbull earnestly strived in response to God's call to service, to resolve the paradoxes of determinism and freedom, and of rationalism and piety. Throughout the notes there prevails a sense of sin and an expression of unworthiness, and of a definite call to witness to the faith and of a passion to win the whole world for the Kingdom.

Sunday, November 1st, 1840

This day I complete twenty-one years spent in this world, and how little I have accomplished thus far for my God or my fellowmen or myself!

It has been communion today -- but my heart was very cold, my view of sin indistinct, my love to the Savior small and poor. During the last month I have spoken to some Christians on religious things -- to three non-professing: Wright of my class, Arthur and Mr. Dodge of the freshman class. This is a poor record to render to my Savior, who died for me, though my studies have crowded me much I might still have done more in the vineyard of my Master.

My spirit of prayer has been too dull. Oh that I might feel the danger of souls around me! Lord open my eyes and warm my heart -- for my own family I have felt some warmth; the thought of their living and dying God's enemies' awakens some feeling. In regard to some of them the reply of Jesus to his disciples comes to my mind "this kind goes not out but by fasting and prayer," I am therefore resolved to fast tomorrow and pray for their conversion and for my own heart to be melted and warmed.

David Trumbull

Sunday, November 8, 1840

Cold, cold heart, sometimes skeptical doubts crowd upon my mind -- of all shapes and tho usually they do not continue in such strength, their influence leads to deadening religious ardor, and to offer excuses for inactivity. I feel myself to be at fault in knowing so little of my Bible's content or the proof of authenticity.

D.T.

Monday, March 14, 1841

There is much religious interest in college now. Many have been led to ask the way of life -- for which I praise God. There have been twenty-five or thirty who think they have been pious -- time will try them. God grant that it may not end here -- there are still two hundred impenitent and I wish all might come in.

My own course for the first year has been strange, sad and sinful. I am guilty in not having prayed more for and warned my friends of their danger -- in not having more at heart the glory of God. I have not honored my Savior among men by my holy example, and should I meet them tonight in Judgment their blood is on my skirts. O God help me to weep over this! -- may my heart so insensible be made to feel -- show me what I am -- bring my sins before my eyes and make me humble!

There have been, as we hope, eight or nine conversions in our class -- and not one in the southern Division. Something is wrong and perhaps it is I. Tis certain I have been a hindrance but O Lord, if so, now help me to remove the obstacle or remove it Thyself -- but suffer me not to impede the work!

Almighty God my Father -- I would like to make the following solemn confession -- and write it that it may be before my eyes to warn me in the future --

For the portion of my life prior to becoming pious I was a wicked sinner and after having had pious teaching in childhood, had become a profane swearer, a sabbath breaker and a hater of God, and had said even with my lips -- I will not now have Thee to reign over me.

By thy grace and faithfulness of a Christian family I was, as I hope, induced to become pious. Now I have not since becoming a professor, been the Christian that I ought; my standard has been too low -- and I have said in my example, peace to the wicked. Having vowed all to Christ I have kept back a part -- I have neglected to study the Bible, to converse with sinners, to pray for them as was my duty. My heart sins are many, pride has risen against Thee, and my love has been much on the world. Now I wish to come back to Thee, to whom I have been false, whom I have dishonored before men by trifling and ill-timed mirth, whom I have not loved with my whole heart. And owning that sin do profess repentance and ask pardon -- in class whom I have wounded -- and I do here solemnly dedicate myself to thy will as long as I live, to pray for Thy kingdom, and to labor and to promote it, seeking opportunities to converse with sinners and in all things imitate my Savior's example . . . Now, O God, I am weak, keep thou me, and let me not wander away, but keep me to be a man of prayer and always a humble active Christian.

David Trumbull(8)

In the wake of revivalism and the theological controversy, Yale College became a center of Home and Foreign

Missions. The American Board of Commissioners for Foreign Missions was organized in the home of Professor Moses Stuart, and the first three presidents were Yale men.(9) The first annual meeting of the American Board of Commissioners for Foreign Missions was held at Farmington, Connecticut (1810) in the home of Noah Porter (1811-1892), professor in Yale College and president from 1871-1886.(10) Jeremiah Evarts (1781-1831) of the class of 1807 became the distinguished correspondence secretary of the American Board and editor of its publication "The Missionary Herald." He issued the call for the students of his day in the words:

> There are in our country young men enough to carry forward the work of missions to an indefinite extent; young men of undoubted piety, qualified to rank high in their several callings as evangelists, pastors, founders of rising churches, translators of the Bible, directors of the press, teachers of children and youths, magistrates of colonies in their incipient state, husbandmen, mechanics of every useful occupation and seamen of every class, from the experienced navigator, who can guide his gallant ship in the unknown waters, to the hardy sailor who is willing to buffet the waves of every ocean and run the hazard of every climate. Persons of all these descriptions stand ready, and wait only for the word from our churches to go forth into all lands and proclaim the unsearchable riches of Christ to the ends of the world. (11)

Such a call to the young men of Yale College did not fall on deaf ears. Peter Parker (1804-1888) of the class of 1831 went out from the Center of Student Religious Activities to Canton, China, commissioned by the American Board in 1834, thus to become the father of medical missions and the beginnings of the Yale-in-China Mission.(12) Hiram Bingham (1831-1908), class of 1853, was a leader of the College Missionary Society. This Phi Beta Kappa-football-scholar and athlete went as a pioneer missionary to the peoples of the Hawaiian Islands and was distinguished as a translator of the Scriptures.(13)

In view of the purpose of the founding fathers of Yale College it is not surprising that half of the graduates went into the ministry at home or abroad. In the *Record* of May 1887 David Trumbull calls attention to this data. Little did he dream in his undergraduate days that he himself would be the pioneer of a Yale-in-Chile.(14)

With all his pessimistic introspection David Trumbull made a positive and pleasing impression upon those who came in contact with him. One who knew him in college wrote:

While here, the connection of his family with that of the elder Professor Silliman gave him exceptional opportunities for making the best use of the advantages offered by the college. . . We cannot refrain from alluding to what we ourselves remember of the impression that he made upon those who came in contact with him. In all that he did or said there was displayed a certain nobility of character which was more attractive as it seemed so natural to him. He had a rich vein of humor; and we will add -- as it seems to have been a characteristic that was often made a subject of remark wherever he went during all his life -- his face wore a peculiarly joyous expression which was quite remarkable, and gave an additional charm to the genial smile with which he always greeted those to whom he spoke. Yet the impression which he gave to all was that of a man of marked independence of character, and no one could even doubt that he possessed, and would retain through life, the full courage of his convictions.(15)

Having spent his college days in the cradle of New England liberal theology, it may seem strange that David Trumbull prepared for the Christian ministry at the Presbyterian Theological Seminary. The two institutions were in the midst of a theological controversy which was to last for forty years and to disrupt both the Congregational and the Presbyterian Churches. For the Old School Calvinists at Princeton, Talorism of the Yale Divinity School was a pernicious and divisive heresy.(16) Yet in spite of it all there was a certain predestination in the enrollment of David Trumbull at Princeton. In his Journal of September 18, 1842 we read:

Princeton Theological Seminary is my present location. In 1837 my way was blocked up completely, and I was put in the way of study -- then brought to join the people of God; and doubting as to my future course, then had my resources cut off; then received the kind offer of Mr. Backus of a scholarship and here I am to use it.

If the guiding hand of God to whom my grandmother Tunis and my mother carried me in dedication and prayer so often, is not shown here -- what could show it? Delightful thought that he guides my course -- Still, Lord, direct and give me a disposition to follow they leadings! I pray for trusting too much in intellectual ability and feeling pride in religious experiences. I have reason to mourn over low grade of action.

Am now preparing to be a minister of the Savior -- an awful responsibility -- to understand Christianity -- to view the human race in the light of the Bible -- to see man's dangers and needs, then to bring them God's own message! What words can tell the minister's burden! What piety, wisdom, earnestness, prayer, acquaintance with God and man are needed! Who is sufficient for these things? O God fit me and guide me!(17)

November 1842 the Journal continues:

This morning's discourse was on "The Glorious Gospel" and the need of proclaiming it, and the required characteristics of the proclaimer. This afternoon the subject was "The doctrine of Providence." If we allow that there is a God, and that He, God, either in the light of the Scriptures or the guidance of reason, the true conclusion seems to be a constant and particular providence, but a practical scepticism saps the influence of this, and indeed, constant views of the divine hand in every passing event is only the attendant of much piety. The more devoted the christian, and the closer he dwells to his God, the more he feels the reality and consolation of this doctrine. He who obsesses Providence will have obsessive days, thus in the future I will be more careful to note passing events, and by the recurrence to the past strive to banish the neglect of seeing His hand, so insulting to God and harmful to myself.(18)

February 6, 1845.

This day begins the sixth Christian year of my life. Last theological session is now within three months of its close. Feel the lack of personal heart experience in Paul's Epistles.(19)

It was indeed providential that David Trumbull should prepare for the ministerial vocation having been influenced by the liberal tradition of New England and the orthodox tradition of Princeton Seminary. Both schools contributed a sound and well-balanced education of one well equipped to minister to the moral and spirtual needs of peoples facing the anxieties of social and political change. In retrospect the "Established Disciplines" of Princeton Theological Seminary seemed peculiarly suited to the future exigencies of the agent of the Reformed faith in a dominantly Catholic country. The very names of the illustrious professors and the titles of their courses reflect the quality of education of the minister-ial candidate, to wit:

Archibald Alexander, D.D. (1812-1851) Professor of Pastoral and Polemic Theology.
Charles Hodge, D.D. (1822-1878) Professor of Exegetical and Didactic Theology.
Samuel Miller, D.D. (1813-1836) Professor of Ecclesiastical History and Church Government.
Joseph A. Alexander, D.D. (1838-1859) Professor of Oriental and Biblical Literature.
James Waddel Alexander, (1849-1851) Professor of Hermeneutics.
William Henry Green, M.A., Assistant Teacher of the Hebrew Language.

Of this faculty the following estimate is given:

The Education and Call to Service of David Trumbull 39

> In speaking of Dr. Alexander we are not lead away from Dr. Hodge. The two men were only two parts of one whole. We might set the matter thus: Alexander was the Socrates of the Princeton School, and Hodge has proven to be its Plato and Aristotle. The two men between them have been the leading power in eliciting a school of Christian thought, which more and more manifestly is destined to be the dominant thought of Christian America.
>
> The manner of the Princeton School has been peculiar. . .they have in their controversies been ernest, eloquent, warm, even passionate; but as far as we know, they have invariably spoken as true Christian gentlemen, who in relation to adversaries make due allowance for the fact-speaking *more Americano* -- 'there's a good deal of human nature in man.' They have shown themselves to be manly men of heroic type.(20)

Dr. Charles Hodge of the Princeton School was especially helpful in the education of David Trumbull. His three volumes of Systematic Theology were for three years the daily mental diet of David. As editor of the Princeton Review he was esteemed the best living exponent of the Calvinistic System and the Westminster Standards. Dr. Alexander said of him, "he was like John Calvin, without his severity."(21) His magnanimity and forbearance toward those with whom he disagreed were notably manifest in his defense of the validity of Romish Baptism and in affirmation that the Church of Rome is a part of the Visible Church. "To Roman Catholic and Protestant, Dr. Hodge comes with a defense of the common creeds of Christendom . . . He treats Polemics in the Spirit of Irenics."(22)

These characteristics of David Trumbull's beloved teacher were clearly reflected in his student as during the years 1845-1889 he so uniquely pursued the "Errand In the Wilderness" at "the uttermost part of the earth." Judging by the references to him in his Journal and in his own style of living, David seems to have been especially fond of his teacher.

Dr. Hodge was a member of the Presbyterian Board of Foreign Missions in 1846 and was president of the Board in 1868;(23) and no doubt he was especially interested in David's acceptance of the call that came to his student when days of preparation were completed.

Throughout college and seminary days David Trumbull was burdened with a sense of mission, and so when commencement came he gave evidence in his Journal of an agonizing indecision, when a definitive call came to him. He wrote:

September 27, 1844.

A man was much needed in Valparaiso in Chile to preach to Americans there and then find access to the Spanish population. . . and so may God, who has so far guided me, lead me now. . . I will think of it and wait for further communication -- though it would be pleasant to remain in my own land -- but the Gospel should be carried everywhere. "O God make the path clear and fit me to walk in it."

The notes then record debates led by Professors Alexander, Hodges, Joel Hawes and Fitch on "Voluntary Action, Atonement, Socialism, Abolition.

February 12, 1845.

Rose at 6:30 -- prayer before breakfast This is not early enough and yet so little resolution to rise, -- I am put to shame by His earlier hour.

Chopped some wood after breakfast -- ax was dull.

Wrote to Dr. Brigham -- Enclosed $5.00 for the American Bible Society.

Spoke at Trenton on Psalm 40:2.

Had a delightful interview with Dr. Alexander about Valparaiso.

March 24, 1845.

Began a letter to my parents in answer of one from Ma (Eliza Bruen T.) regarding South America. My mind is sorely puzzled on this point. It seems as the field was open there and in some respects as though I am fitted to enter and till it -- and scattering seed to wait patiently for God to give the increase among either the sceptical Englishmen and South Americans or among the superstitious Catholics. Divine Grace -- guide me in thy wonderful mercy -- Thou who hast already rescued my slipping feet from the paths of danger and sin!

In David Trumbull's dossier at Princeton Theological Seminary, in response to an inquiry of the Alumni Secretary, he gave the following information on licensure and ordination:

Licensed in June, 1844 by the New London County Association of Ministers, Connecticut.

Ordained by a Congregational Council convened at Norwich, Conneticut, June 13th, 1845. Dr. Alvin Bond was moderator. Sent to Valparaiso, under the Foreign Evangelical Society (since,

American and Foreign Christian Union) to preach to seafaring men and ultimately to spread the Gospel among the native population. (24)

It was not easy for David Trumbull to set sail for Valparaiso, Chile. Following his Journal we can read between the lines of haunting intimations of mind and spirit, for he wrote for August 1845, the following:

Ship, Mississippi -- Sabbath August 17, my first at sea and being sick -- a heavy dull day. Nothing to say to others and wishing to have mother speaking to me. -- no discontentment, however, nor despondency.

August 24, 1845. This time was able to preach to passengers and crew on deck; Matthew 6:33 (But seek ye first His kingdom and all things shall be yours as well.) May it do some good!

Sabbath, August 31, 1845. Tho felt unwell, still preached, and the execution did me good -- Ephesians 2:12 (you were strangers to the covenants of promise, having no hope and without God in the world) Audience attentive, Mr. Carter hopes seriously that he might become a christian on this voyage -- May he find the cross; and O may I be guided how to move among these men! None seem serious among the passengers.

September 7, 1845

After dinner had a talk with a seaman named Chas. White, an Englishman. Said he had been very wicked -- disgrace to his parents -- away since eight years. I pointed to an atoning Savior as a source of hope and the Holy Spirit as the power who would counsel him -- May the Lord, if he has begun with him, carry him onwards! O may the Almighty God crown my intercourse with these persons with his abounding blessing and convert their souls!

There is more bad feeling among the passengers than I would be pleased to see. C. is very sulky for some reason. My heart is pained to see such indifference to religion among these on board. The language I hear is generally respectful but there is much wordliness and the evil day is put far off. If I might see fruit of God's Spirit moving on these minds and might hear them question for the way of pardon, what pleasure it would afford me! I have some desire to see many brothers enter the family of God -- that they may be saved -- that they may be the means of bringing the truth to others.

Friday, October 31st, 1845

Ship, Mississippi - My 26th birthday is near at hand! a year since, little did I think of spending it here -- but reviewing past life I hope I can see God leading me for good. There is an undercurrent of self conceit in me; and I feel at times as if my efforts in the world were to be effective, and this so much that I seldom think there is a probability of death for a long while.

Now I hope God has given me talents for preaching the Gospel -- indeed from experience I am sure He has; but O may I not become proud of it nor fall into a foolish and wicked self confidence nor into a habit of indolent reliance on natural capacity. Surely a man should judge as candidly as possible concerning his faculties but not under nor overrate them.

Saturday, November 1st, 1845

Another birthday comes around -- now I am 26 years old -- I think my feelings are grateful to Him who has so far led me and kept me -- that I have been guided to a life of study, then to religious study and a ministerial life, I am often reminded of the defective manner in which I have pursued my studies with such superior advantages. I am determined to make this first year of my professional life, one of more mental and spirtual activity than any before it and O may God whom I serve strengthen me thus to do!

The captain tells me that he hears no one on board speak other than well of me; that I have gained the confidence and respect of all. If he is not mistaken I thank God for it and hope He will help me hereafter to be a faithful Christian and let men see that I believe and practive what I say, and O my Father may I enjoy the privilege of winning souls, of some souls to Christ!

Sabbath, November 2, 1845

Slight headache again; Yet I preached in the cabin and had very good attention. Captain said I had given them a good discourse; that it touched him and he felt it. 'Twas on doing good; James 4:17, (He that knoweth to do good and doeth it not -- to him it is sin)

Headache -- sit at Captain's door -- very pleasantly he advises soak feet and a glass of lemonade -- which the steward brot me -- Thank God for His mercies which line my path!

Tuesday, November 18, 1845

Captain Harvey came to my stateroom this morning and I read him my letter of instructions from the Committee of the Foreign Evangelical Society, which speaks of my going to other ports after gaining a knowledge of the language to see how things are and what can be done one way or another. He then urged the usefulness of such a trip and renewed his kind and christian offer of passage free in his ships as a friend of his and offers all his influence in making acquaintances.

November 26, 1845

S.W. of Cape Horn

December 14, 1845

The voyage still lingers, but I hope my old and joking guess will prove correct that by Christmas we shall arrive.

Friday morning, December 19, 1845, Latitude 47°

Dear Parents,
Captain Harvey gave me a very fine, large quarter Bible -- as a present, and with this a complimentary letter signed by himself and the passengers "to Rev. David Trumbull for his kindness in conducting worship on board on the Sabbath."

This is all very well enough but I shall say tonight at Prayers that while I thank them for their kindness -- still they have something more to do besides complimenting Christ's messenger -- to notice and accept the message.

Thursday morning, December 25 - Christmas Day

Valparaiso just in sight twelve miles off. Many of the passengers are already dressed up in their Sunday-go-to-meeting clothes, but I feel that we shall not land before midday five or six hours hence, the wind being very light.

The shore is close -- high, dark bank but with no trees on it -- not very inviting to the eyes -- unlike the neighborhood of our cities, for not a house is to be seen -- how the railroad enterprise will succeed is extremely doubtful! -- but we shall see -- and when ready for passengers, you shall hear. The Captain thinks it will prove all moonshine.

I was kindly received by a committee of the English clergymen -- I must move with caution -- I hope to be unhindered. This, I think, is a well chosen field but not an easy one.

                            David Trumbull

Sabbath, December 21, 1845

This morning did not get up until nearly eight o'clock and missed morning prayer, for which I am sorry.

Wednesday, December 24, 1845

Chiefly engaged about going ashore now. Wind too light for landing, or make harbor tonight; fear I shall not get on shore in time for communion which I long to do.

December 25, 1845

Rose at 4 a.m. as the light came on point of land ahead. Valparaiso -- point -- hills bleak and barren -- not a tree in sight -- save a cactus on a hilltop -- appearance very uninviting.

And thus it was that David Trumbull had a "superior advantage for study" and in his Journals he records for history the intimations from childhood to manhood of a providential call to preach the Gospel in the "Wilderness."

4

FORERUNNERS IN THE VALE OF PARADISE

> *Puro Chile, es tu cielo azulado:*
> *puras brisas te cruzan también,*
> *y tu campo de flores bordado,*
> *es la copia feliz del Edén.*
>
> *Majestuosa es la blanca montaña*
> *que te dio por baluarte el Senor,*
> *y ese mar que tranquilo te baña,*
> *te promete futuro esplendor.*
>
> *(Chile -- land of blue skies --*
> *Of gentle breezes -- land adorned*
> *with flowers, majestic mountains*
> *and tranquil sea --*
> *Thou art a true image of the*
> *Garden of Eden -- the promise*
> *of future splendor.)(1)*

The Most Illustrious Catholic Monarch Charles Vth commissiones his servant, Christopher Columbus, to win souls in the New World and to add more domains to his far-flung kingdom. Diego de Almagro, lieutenant of the uncouth and avaricious Francisco de Pizarro, ventured to cross the bleak desert of Atacama in his avid quest of *El Dorado*. Unwittingly he bypassed the rich deposits of copper and nitrate and turned back north to Lima, the City of the Kings, advising his followers to "shun this land like a plague."(2) But the actual conquistador of Chile, Captain Pedro de Valdivia, gave a different report to his king.

In September of 1545 he wrote:

> . . . and for the information of the merchants and gentry desirious of coming and settling, let them come; because this land is such that to live and remain in it there is no better in the world. I say this because it is very pleasant, most healthy and of much content, having not more than four months of winter . . . The summer is so temperate, and of such delight are the breezes that blow, that a man can go all day in the sun without ill effect. It is most abundant in grasses and sowings suitable to the raising of all manner of stock and crops that may be imagined, much fine timber for building houses, and an infinite variety of woods for the furnishing them; and there are mines of great richness in gold. And all the earth is so generous that wherever they may wish to seek, there shall they find all they require for sowing and for building; and water and kindling, and grazing for their animals, such it appears to have been created by God with the purpose of having all things to hand.(3)

The Quechua Indians of Peru called Chile, "the land where the earth comes to an end." The Spanish conquistadors called it "Nueva Extremadura" in honor of a frontier province in Spain. The Araucanian Indians who lived in this far-away land were indomitable. The story of their heroic defense of their native habitat and their formidable resistance to the Spanish military was recorded in the first Epic Poem of the New World. Alonzo de Ercilla (1533-1595), a young Spanish officer, composed this classical literary work called *La Araucana*. In 2,645 eight line stanzas, Ercilla describes in vivid and rhythmic language the country, the natives and their customs and the strategies of war. He wrote in praise of the valiant and gallant Indians and in criticism of the lustful and haughty Spaniards. In later years the Chilean people were proud of this double heritage of daring adventure and love of freedom and inscribed on their coat-of-arms the motto "Por la Razon o Fuerza" (By Reason or Force).

In keeping with the optimistic reports to their king, the Spaniards founded, in the year 1544, a village on the coast of central Chile. They called it Valparaiso (Vale of Paradise). By the dawn of the nineteenth century this obscure hamlet became a thriving city of 30,000 inhabitants, 6,000 of whom were English-speaking. Remarkable changes had occured which made this community one which was much more like the place described by Pedro de Valdivia -- a veritable Garden of Eden. There were certain forerunners who were agents of this change and who prepared the way for the man from New England.

Latin America Precursors

The Hispanic heritage of the provinces of the king in the New World was of inestimable value, yet in many ways it proved to be a barrier to the socioeconomic and political development of communities made up of native and popular elements which were destined to create different ways of living. Two contemporary authors offer keys to the understanding of the development of Chilean society. Alberto Edwards Vives, in his book "La Fronda Aristocractica (The Aristocratic Branch), finds the touchstone of Chilean socioeconomic and political phenomena in the adroit assumption by the landed aristocracy of the roles formerly played by the Spanish Crown and that of the Church. Even though the new nation adopted a Republican form of government, the traditional social structures of the long colonial period prevailed.

On the other hand, historian Ricardo Donoso, in his book "Las Ideas Politícas en Chile" (The Political Ideas in Chile), finds the key to the development of Chilean society in the struggle to liberate the new nation from the traditional hierarchical and oligarchical dominance. With cogent and candid documentation, the author traces the trends toward the achievement of an egalitarian society and representative government. These ideologies, according to Ricardo Donoso, were inspired by the Enlightenment, the American and French Revolutions, the influence of international trade and travel and, not least, by the influence of diplomatic agents of the United States.

The confrontation of these differing ideologies created tensions so disruptive as to give rise to the civil wars of 1830, 1839, 1851, 1859, and 1891. These conflicts were also the underlying causes of the tensions between Church and State and were the basic issues involved in the constitutional Reforms of the 1860's and the 1870's. The Independence Movement of 1810-1825 was a violent reaction against the monopolistic and restrictive rule of the mother country. The aspirations for self-identity and freedom of the emerging nation-state are cogently expressed by the motto of the University of Concepción in southern Chile -- "For the Free Unfolding of the Spirit."

Religious tolerance and freedom of worship were advocated by some of the founding fathers of the new Republic. However, the conservative party, after much debate, succeeded in formulating Article V of the constitution as follows: "The Religion of the State is the Roman Catholic Apostolic to the exclusion of the public worship of all others."(4) In order to affirm the national autonomy, the United States Minister, Joel Poinsett, suggested the elimination of the word "Roman", but to no avail.

Fray Henrique Camilo, a liberal priest, steeped in the ideology of Voltaire and Rousseau, denounced the monarchical system of government and zealously advocated a representative form of government, popular education and a free press. He recommended to the Supreme Director of Chile, Don Bernardo O'Higgins, the Lancastrian system of education. The Supreme Director claimed for Chile the right of National Patronage which would effectively control the Church. Fearing his dictatorial powers and objecting to his liberal innovations, the landed-aristocracy, allied with the military and the Church, forced O'Higgins to abdicate. Soon after he went into voluntary exile to Peru and died there in 1836. Fray Henrique Camilo was also exiled for his daring support of popular sovereignty and democratic rule. Much later these two founding fathers of the nation were reincorporated into the annals of the nation and now are universally venerated as heroes.

Andres Bello (1781-1865), although a Venezuelan by birth, had a profound influence on the cultural formation of the Chilean nation. Mentor of Simón Bolívar, he accompanied the Liberator to England in order to seek aid for the Independence Movement. After spending eighteen years in London he was engaged in 1829 by the Chilean ambassador to serve as Chile's Secretary of Foreign Affairs. He organized in 1842 the University of Chile, following as a model the autonomous structure of the University of Paris. He was the first Rector of the University. In 1855 he wrote the Civil Code for the nation, incorporating the principles of constitutional government.(5) He was the co-author of one of the first grammars of the Spanish language. Stressing as he did the need for classical education, he molded the character of a new generation of Chilean youth who were destined to bring about far-reaching changes in the traditional ways of the Spanish heritage. Two of these disciples, José Victorino Lastarria (1817-1888) and Francisco Bilbao (1823-1865), supported the Black Legend theory -- the view that Spain and Roman Catholicism were responsible for the backwardness of the Latin American nations.(6) Lastarria was an ardent advocate of Positivism and a pioneer of the sociological approach to cultural understanding. These ideologies gave rise to secularity and scientific humanism, which only abetted the conflict between Church and State.

Francisco Bilbao was singularly a precursor of David Trumbull. His biographer calls him "a true saint in the annals of republican America".(7) Because of his progressive ideas and open criticism of the Church and State, he was driven into exile in 1844 to Peru and France.

While in France he met Félicité Robert de Lamennais (1782-1854) an ardent advocate of political democracy and church renewal.

Bilbao became an enthusiastic disciple of Lamennais. He translated his mentor's books, *On Modern Slavery*, *The Words of a Believer*, and *The Gospels*. Upon reading his *Book of the People*, Bilbao wrote, "since then my young mind was exposed to the light which illuminated the pages of Ercilla's *Araucana* and confirmed for me the scientific certitude of the eternal republicanism, which was taught to me by my father and was reflected in the struggle for independence of my country".(8) The Chilean student also accepted the teachings of Lamennais concerning religious tolerance, the separation of Church and State, freedom of expression, the freedom of assembly and universal suffrage.(9)

Returning to Chile in 1850 Bilbao became an apostle for social justice and freedom. "More than ever", wrote his biographer, "his one desire was to agitate the people and preach the revolution against the traditionalists".(10) In 1864 he published his book, *The American Gospel*. In it he traced the history of truth and justice and its application to the cultures of South and North America. He envisioned a continental congress which would promote international laws, the abolition of customs duties, universal education and intellectual cooperation.(11) Seen in historical perspective his ideas proved to be prophetic, as indeed was his retort to the judge who condemned his critical essay, *Sociabilidad Chilena* (the Nature of Chilean Society), with the words, "the eternal philosophical code will classify me as an innovator, but you, senor juez (judge), as a retrogade official".(12) Once again the former exile was repatriated. Today his name adorns the streets and plazas of almost every village and city in the republic.

Domingo Faustino Sarmiento (1811-1888), a native of Argentina, was exiled by the tyrant Juan Manuel de Rosas (1793-1877). He spent fifteen years in Chile and, although a self-educated man, he achieved renown as "the school-master-president". In Chile he was a school teacher, a shop clerk, a mine foreman and a newspaper journalist. President Manuel Montt commissioned him to study North American and European school systems in order to establish elementary schools in Chile. While in the United States he became acquainted with Horace Mann, whose wife translated Sarmiento's classical book, *Facundo: Civilization versus Barbarism*. Returning to Chile, Sarmiento became an advocate of the North American system of education. He founded the Normal School in

1842, which to this day bears his name. He wrote readers for the elementary grades which served as the text books for several generations of Chileans. Education of the masses was for him the only hope for a true democracy and cultural progress. Rather than limit teaching to the elite, as Andres Bello was prone to do, Sarmiento was in favor of practical instruction suited to the native characteristics and vocational needs of the developing nation. This emphasis was the beginning of a literary genre called "Criollism" (Creolism) -- an interest in creating a *sui generis* culture. Sarmiento was ambassador from Argentina to the United States in 1855. From 1868-1874 he was president of his country. While president he contracted eighty-six North American school teachers to organize the school system in Argentina. In all these endeavors he was a precursor of David Trumbull in intercultural relations north and south.

Anglo-Saxon Forerunners

"You shall be my witnesses unto the uttermost part of the earth." (Acts I;8)

Henry Hill (1795-1892) was born at Newburg, New York, and was raised in the village of Catskill-on-the-Hudson. His home was the Meeting House for the Protestant community. He learned all about the Bible in the Sunday School and was disciplined in the austerity of his parent's thriving business. His motto was, "In each event of life how clear, Thy ruling hand I see". He was destined to establish the first North American business firm in Valparaiso, Chile. As representative of several agencies and owners of North American shipping vessels he made a fortune during the years 1817-1820 by selling supplies and weapons of war to the Chilean patriots in their Independence Movement 1810-1825. Having been appointed Consul of the United States for Santiago and Valparaiso, he mingled freely with the Liberators and the leading citizens of the country. In 1822 Henry Hill returned to his native land and became a member of the American Board of Commissioners for Foreign Missions and after thirty-two years as treasurer of the Board he served for eleven years as a member of the Prudential Committee of the same organization. In his *Recollection of an Octogenarian*, supplemented by information from his Chilean biographer, we are presented with the image of our first Anglo-Saxon forerunner of David Trumbull. Chilean historian Eugenio Pereira Salas writes:

> Henry Hill was a perfect type of the North American at the beginning of the century; he was firmly rooted in the Puritan tradition

which limited the spiritual heritage to a narrow and strict morality; yet on the other hand encouraged the spirit of adventure, the zeal for business, the demand for profits, which were psychologically signs of triumph of the capitalistic order over the traditional structure. Romanticism and pragmatic action were both a part of his personality. While he was undertaking questionable armament deals, at the same time he was writing in romantic terms about his Puritan Catskill village. Later in the midst of holocaust and violence, which emerged from the revolutionary struggles, he counted these as nothing in comparison to the unbroken attachment he maintained to his ascetic lover Beatriz of his native village.

In his later years, in order to atone for his mistaken achievements and endeavors, he dedicated his entire time to plant the cross of Christ in the Araucanian wilderness.

The life of Henry Hill ordinarily might have been of little significance but in his threefold role as business man, vice-consul and missionary he was related to some important episodes, such as the provision of armaments in support of the revolution: he was also a witness to the establishment of the Republic, and in the history of economics he figures as the founder of the first North American business firm in Chile.(13)

Henry Hill was agent for the Frigate *Macedonia*. This ship protected the North American commerce routes along the west coast of South America during the war with Spain. One of our ships was confiscated by Admiral Lord Cochran who was in charge of the Chilean navy. As Consul, Henry Hill was deeply involved with the subsequent international litigation of this affair, but this was not so much a problem to him as was the problem presented by the following episode:

> Mr. Wilson, the chaplain of the *Macedonia* died on shore while at Valparaiso, Chile. An application to deposit the remains at the beautiful cemetary there was made to the principle ecclesiastic. Was he a Catholic? "No," I said "but he was a christian minister and an officer of our Navy." All my statements and arguments were of no avail. The old Canon would be most happy to do everything in his power, but the Church allowed burial only to Roman Catholics. I then went to the Governor who most cheerfully offered any ground over which the Government had control. He stated that the arsenal was their finest building, and the enclosure was surrounded by a high wall and this was free from any danger of molestation. This place was decided upon. Captain Basil Hall of the British sloop-of-war *Conway* attended the funeral with such of his officers as could be spared, and his marines fired a volley over the grave. He had previously sent a half a dozen of his sailors in their blue jackets and white trousers, with spades to assist in digging the grave and in carrying the body.(14)

Henry Hill, merchant, consul and missionary returned to the United States in March of 1821. His former business partner of the firm Lynch-Hill Company wrote to urge him to return to South America in order to take advantage of the new markets in Peru, which country was recently freed from Spain by Liberator San Martin, but Henry Hill gave up his economic and political roles to dedicate himself to his missionary vocation as he himself wrote:

> In the year 1821 I returned from abroad. My wife and I were seeking for treasure which could not be found in Peru. She was endeavoring to raise one thousand dollars for foreign missions and I was assisting her in that laudable undertaking. This and my desire that missionaries should be sent to South America, led me to correspond with Mr. Evarts and Dr. Anderson and acquaindance with other friends of missions. In 1822 I became treasurer of the American Board for Commissioners for Foreign Missions and so continued until 1854. For eleven years I was a member of the Prudential Committee of that Board; nearly nine years I was treasurer of the American Tract Society, Boston..(15)

While treasurer of the American Board, Don Estanislao Lynch wrote the following note to his former business partner:

> Lima, Sept. 8, 1822
>
> The British and Foreign Bible Society sent me at your recommendation 500 Spanish Bibles and 500 Spanish Testaments, all of which were disposed of -- either sold or given away in less than three days.(16)

Missionary Henry Hill, much like his successor, David Trumbull, believed in predestination for his closing words of his "Recollections" were, "After three times accidentally falling into the water before learning to swim, it surely becomes me to say, 'The life which Thou hast made Thy care, Lord, I devote to Thee'."(17)

The second Anglo-Saxon forerunner of David Trumbull was James Thompson (1778-1854) a Scotsman. He was a lay representative of the British and Foreign Bible Society and also of the Lancasterian School Society. He was invited by Bernardo O'Higgins to promote popular education in Chile. The decree in support of the Lancasterian Schools was as follows:

> The Lancastrian system of mutual instruction, now introduced in most parts of the civilized world, and to which many places already owe an improvement in their habits, has been established among us and is such a manner as gives promise of beneficial results. The propagation of this system holds out the surest

means of extirpating those principles formed among us in times of darkness. The government has resolved to protect this establishment zealously and, as the best way of fulfilling its intentions, has resolved to unite it in its object those persons who, at the same time, possess that activity, zeal and energy which this important matter demands . . . Of this Society I will be the protector and a member. The solicitor general of city, the protector of the schools and the rector of the National Institute will be members ex-oficio of the committee of management.

The object of this Society will be to extend throughout Chile the benefits of education, to promote the instruction of all classes but especially the poor, and to point out those means by which it may be best adapted to the circumstances and necessities of the country.

Signed, Bernardo O'Higgins (19)

Citizen Thompson urged the Government to invite foreign traders and agriculturalists to come to Chile in order to promote the economic development of the new Republic. But the clerical party strongly objected to his schools and the entrance of non-Roman Catholics stating that such innovations would destroy the cultural unity of the nation. Friar Guzman, reporting for an ecclesiastical commission stated:

It would not be prudent to receive these devouring vipers who are not Roman Catholics into the bosom of the State which desires to conserve pure, clean and inviolable the religion which it confesses. The coming to Chile of foreign families would ruin the Catholic religion. One such who pretends to live here should content himself with the tolerance or civil permission which the government has granted to all foreigners to carry on business, free from molestation in regards to their morals and dogmas, provided they do not preach them nor otherwise interfere in religious matters; for in such case they should be expelled as disturbers of the peace, public order and tranquility. (20)

On November 19, 1822 a major earthquake devastated much of central Chile. More than two hundred people lost their lives in Valparaiso. Zealous Catholics interpreted this disaster as a punishment of God because the government permitted the non-Catholics to enter the country. (21)

When James Thompson arrived in Chile in June, 1821, he brought with him sixty copies of the New Testament -- a Spanish edition. The ecclesiastical authorities challenged his right to bring such Testaments into the country. When, however, Thompson explained that he had come to Chile under contract with the Government, the books were admitted. Andres Bello, minister of Foreign Affairs and author of Chile's Civil Code, advocated the suppression of the clerical control of books imported into Chile, but this reform was not approved until 1878.(22) Opposition to the endeavors of James Thompson was a setback for popular education and to a general knowledge concerning the Scriptures. In spite of the initial success of the system of schools he established, after a few years hardly a trace of them was to be found. After residing in Chile for less than a year, James Thompson proceeded north to Peru and to Colombia where he was warmly welcomed by the Latin American Liberators, San Martín and Bolívar, and where his success in establishing the Lancastrian system of schools and the sales of the Scriptures was greater and more permanent than he had achieved in Buenos Aires or in Santiago, Chile.(23)

Another pioneer who set the stage for David Trumbull was John C. Brigham (1794-1862), a native of New Marlborough, Massachusetts.(24) After graduation from Williams College in 1819 and from Andover Theological Seminary in 1822, he was sent with Theophilus Parvin by the American Board of Commissioners for Foreign Missions to explore the Latin American field. Their instructions read as follows:

> Their inquiries will relate to every subject which will have a bearing on the moral and religious state of the people. They will endeavor to ascertain whether the Bible can be freely distributed: how it is received; what is the effect on its introduction among those who never before possessed it; whether tracts could be circulated, and would be read; what is the progress of education among the common people; what are their circumstances; how they regard improvements; in what manner will they receive religious instruction; how far the principles of religious toleration are likely to prevail; and what are the most eligible places for making evangelical exertions of a permanent character. They will probably be able to make arrangements for the distribution of Bibles and tracts from depositories, which can be regularly supplied hereafter.(25)

Parvin and Brigham arrived in Buenos Aires, Argentina on October 24, 1823. They both remained there for a year, occupying the time learning Spanish, in ministering to the Protestant population in that city, in distribution of Bibles and tracts, and in gathering information on the Plata country and its inhabitants.(26)

Parvin established a permanent Evangelical Community in Buenos Aires but when the restrictions of travel due to the Revolutionary wars were lifted, John Brigham proceeded to Chile by way of Mendoza, arriving there in October of 1824. In the few months he was there he made a study of the religious customs and conditions of the people, including the Araucanian Indians in the south and the city of Coquimbo in northern Chile, before going on to Peru, Colombia and Mexico. In his report to the American Bible Society in 1826 John Brigham said:

> Throughout the long road from Buenos Aires to Chile (fourteen days trip), excepting a very few in Mendoza, not a solitary book of God was found and I more than once presented copies to aged priests tottering over the grave who told me they had never before seen it in their native tongue . . . the great mass of people are yet destitute and generally in the interior they never saw, and in some cases they told me they never knew that the Scriptures existed in their own language.(27)

Reporting to the American Board of Commissioners for Foreign Missions Brigham wrote:

> The schools which Mr. Thompson established two years ago in Santiago, Chile have become extinct. There is little prospect of immediately introducing one similar to that of Mr. Parvin in Buenos Aires.
>
> During the few months passed in Chile and Peru I was able to exert little direct religious influence, except in private conversation, and in distributing the Scriptures. In these two ways of doing good I always found much to do, both in places mentioned and afterwards in Colombia and in Mexico; and might have done far more, had I possessed more time and more copies of the sacred volume.(28)
>
> The great reforming work, which they most need, which they must have, or fail in their undertaking is the Bible. Owing to Spanish and Papal policy, few of these sacred books have ever found their way among them, until the last five years; and even now, there are not ten thousand copies among fifteen millions of subjects. There are yet thousands of families who never saw a leaf of this book, and who though baptized in the name of Christ, are never actuated by, and scarcely know a precept which he taught. Can such a people, think you, long enjoy civil freedom, and its attendant blessings?. . . I would repeat it again and again, and would write it on the sky over their heads, that without a wide difusion of the Scriptures, the South Americans will never become so enlightened and purified, that their long blinded communities can be trusted with the right of general suffrage. . .
>
> But, after all our theories of general intellegence, public virtue, free circulation of the Scriptures, and other requisites of a free government, we must remember, that they will all fail unless the Ruler of nations guide and bless the whole. It is the belief that God is moving in that revolution, fulfilling the promise that the kingdoms of this world shall become the kingdom

of our Lord, and his Christ, which more than all things else, inspires the hope, that the change will be effective and glorious. In all the great rapid scenes, of which this continent has, for three centuries been the theater, I cannot but view them as parts of one mighty, infinitely wise design. Through this vast and fertile hemisphere, capable of sustaining many hundred millions of our species, the Governor of the world appears to be preparing the way for a new and happier organization of civil society, as well as for a wider extension, and brighter triumphs, of the kingdom of grace.(29)

In answer to the question of the advisability of direct and open Protestant preaching John Brigham wrote:

The answer is that they could *not* at present. Such a measure, in most places would be opposed as yet to articles of their constitutions, and would create such excitement among the lower orders, that the most liberal enlightened statesmen would discourage it.

Although there are many individuals in South America who have noble and expanded views, men who are up with the spirit of the age, still there is in that field a putrid mass of superstition, on which the sun of liberty must shine still longer before we can safely enter in and labor.(30)

Professor Oliphant closes his study of the Parvin-Brigham Mission to Latin America with the following tribute:

Very definitely the door to Protestant Missionary enterprise in Spanish-America was *not yet* open. Yet there was a long-time effect of the Parvin-Brigham Mission to Spanish-America which should not be lost sight of in the upsurge of early disillusionment. The end was not yet. With the passing of the years new happenings provided material for additional chapters of the history of Protestant missionary activity in Latin America. Never again was Latin America *terra incognita* to the churches in the United States; never during their long years of relative inactivity in that region after 1830 did Christians in the United States completely lose their interest in their southern neighbors . . . Nor could the American Bible Society forget that it had very early assumed particular obligations with respect to Latin America.(31)

Upon his return to the United States, John C. Brigham accepted the invitation to become the Corresponding Secretary of the American Bible Society, a post he occupied until his death in 1862. He was also chairman of the Executive Committee of the America Seamen's Friend Society. He recommended the establishment of, chaplaincies, Seamen's Friend Societies, and depositories for the

Forerunners in the Vale of Paradise 57

distribution of the Scriptures in the several Republics of Latin America. No doubt he and William Wheelwright recruited David Trumbull for service in Chile in 1845, while the latter was finishing his studies at Princeton Seminary in 1845. In Jane Fitch's Journal mention is made of the Rev. John C. Brigham who, in July of 1845, came to say 'goodbye' to David and Jane Trumbull when they went aboard the ship *Crescent City* for Panama and gave them a Spanish New Testament. In any event Brigham wrote the commission to David Trumbull on behalf of the American and Foreign Gospel Society and the American Seamen's Friend Society. (32)

Another forerunner of David Trumbull in the Vale-of-Paradise was William Wheelwright (1798-1873). Born at Newburryport, Massachusetts, he was a descendant of Puritan forebears who settled in the 1630's in New England and was brought up in the best of the Protestant tradition. He was educated at Andover Academy, Massachusetts, being a member of the class of 1814. This young man was destined to change the entire pattern of commerce and communications of the South American Continent. This he did with a rare combination of practical skills with an idealism which won for him the reputation of being "quixotic." From cabin boy he soon advanced to captain of the tradeship *Rising Star* which unfortunately was shipwrecked near Buenos Aires, Argentina in 1823.

In 1824 Wheelwright was engaged in trade on the Pacific coast of South America and settled down in Guayaquil, Ecuador where he lived for five years. During this time he served as consul for the United States. In 1829 he transferred his residence to Valparaiso, Chile, a trading center, which in time he did much to make more like a "Vale-of-Paradise" -- an emporium for the whole western coast of South America. In 1839 he established a trade route from Valparaiso to Panama which later was organized as "The Pacific Steam and Navigation Company." To operate the steamships he searched for and discovered coal in Southern Chile giving rise to the entire mining industry. He improved harbors along the coast by building iron moles and installing buoys and beacons. He promoted international trade by formulating rules and regulations for the prevention of collisions at sea. In 1850 Wheelwright built the first railroad on the Pacific coast of North and South America. This was a stretch of fifty miles constructed to export gold and silver from the mines in Copiapó (northern Chile) to the port of Caldera. At his own expense he surveyed the railroad route from Valparaiso to Santiago. Later he built the trunk-line in Argentina from Rosario to Cordoba with the intention of uniting Argentina and Chile by way of a transndean line.

For Valparaiso he built the first gas works and potable water system. He introduced the telegraph system uniting Valparaiso with the capital city of Santiago.

William Wheelwright accomplished all these achievements in the face of incredulity, vexations of delays, and scarcity of funds at a time when the several Republics were emerging from a war economy. Yet he was enthusiastically supported by the presidents and leaders of the nations. His biographer, J. B. Alberdi, minister of Argentina to France and England, records the esteem and gratitude of the city of Valparaiso with these words:

> . . . Valparaiso, the city perhaps more than all others benefited by his energies and industry, has not shown herself ungrateful to his memory. His full-length portrait has long graced the walls of her Merchants' Exchange and now the Board of Trade has ordered a costly statue in bronze which shall represent him for all time to come, so that prosperity may behold in the public plaza the man to whom it is indebted for so much of its civilization and prosperity. Well may South America place laurels of the brows of her heroes of peace. They are the true soldiers of American liberty in modern times; they form the sacred legion of Washington, who turned his sword into a plowshare the day he concluded the great war of his country's independence.(33)

Alberdi pays tribute to the idealism and Puritan heritage of William Wheelwright with these words:

> Wheelwright is the ideal of the character needed by South America to enoble her to emulate the progress of that society of which he was a native citizen. Representing progress, because he represents steam and electricity applied as forces to the service of man, he represents a superior force, without which his works, however important, would be in comparison of little value-probity, uprightness, honor in industry. . . He was sterling manhood in the service of humanity.(34)

> Faithful to the example of his ancestors, who made a resource of every obstacle, he reflected that if calms were prejudicial to sailing vessels they would be an immense advantage to steamers. (35)

The role of the Scriptures in the formation of the character of William Wheelwright and also its importance for religious teaching is pointed out by Ambassador Alberdi in the following observation.

> At the present day, when public opinion is in favor of discarding all religious teaching and even rejecting the use of the Bible in public schools, it may be well for us to consider the probable effect upon character which either method may produce. No one

can peruse these pages, either in translation or in what has been added to it, without conclusively attributing the success of Mr. Wheelwright, the happiness he enjoyed and which he confered upon nations, to the instruction which he received in his boyhood, and which was mainly derived from the sacred Scriptures. He was taught to regard them with the utmost reverence, his secular knowledge was all based upon them; and when he went out into the world he was thus fortified against its snares and temptations, so that his character as a man was formed out of a ground-work of New England orthodoxy and a super-structure of the knowledge of mankind.(36)

This relevance of religious faith to the secular super-structure is evident in the words of Wheelwright:

> I dare not speak of the electric telegraph, because the more I reflect upon this mighty and wonderful agent, the more inclined I am to be wholly silent. It seems as if the Great God had loaned us this mysterious element in order to fulfill the words of Holy Writ which fortell a period of the reunion of all nations in one brotherhood, when there shall be 'peace on earth and good-will to men.'(37)

William Wheelwright was an active agent of the Reformed Church in Latin America. David Trumbull wrote of him:

> He felt a warm interest in all that favored education and was anxious to promote the moral and religious welfare of the American and English resident of this coast. He procured, entirely at his own expense the material for the church which was erected at Callao (Peru) for Protestants and sent them around Cape Horn.(38)

His home was a depository for the Bible Societies and a residence for the colporteur Luke Matthews who it was feared fell victim to his zeal in circulating the Scriptures in the mountain passes of Chimborazo.(39) His brother, Isaac Watts Wheelwright, was appointed in 1833 as the first agent for the American Bible Society "to make a determined effort to put the Spanish Scriptures in circulation in Chile and in fact, in all the coast regions as far north as the western slopes of Mexico."(40)

A fellow-engineer sums up this brief account of the Anglo-Saxon precursor of David Trumbull with the following tribute:

> The study of men like Wheelwright and striving to become like them, is the true way to introduce and acclimatize, in South America, and to the advantage of the Latin race, Saxon liberty and Saxon progress A hero of peace-which means progress-he was also a representative of even greater virtues, without which

industry and its results are of slight value. He was a man of
truth, uprightness and sobriety. Luxury would have been but a
torment to his simple tastes; the luxury in which he took delight
was that of doing good to his fellow-being. The teaching of
Christianity was apparent in all his actions.(41)

By way of "teaching of Christianity," Wheelwright gave
substantial gifts of money "for the translation of the
Scriptures into the Turkish language and for the promotion and propagating of Christianity in the Far East."
He also endowed a school in his native town of Newburyport,
Massachusetts, for the technical education of Protestant
youth.(42)

5

THE REFORMED CHURCH IN THE WILDERNESS

Timothy Dwight, President of Yale College from 1795 to 1817, wrote the words of the hymn:

> I love thy Church, O God:
> Her walls before Thee stand,
> Dear as the apple of Thine eye,
> And graven on Thy hand.
>
> For her my tears shall fall,
> For her my prayers ascend;
> To her my cares and toils be given,
> Till toils and cares shall end.

    The purpose of the College, said President Dwight, was, "to train men for service in a community dedicated to God as Governor". The hymn and the purpose thus expressed served as an inspiration and guideline for David Trumbull who was to spend forty years as minister of a pilgrim people in something of a wilderness. In letters to his family back home he wrote:

> The country is all hills, hills, hills, with gullies intervening, caused probably by earth quakes. The name of the place means Valley of Paradise -- but the idea of Paradise must have been low to have given such a spot such a name. . . . the first night I came on shore a slight shock of an earthquake was felt -- but none since. The sensation was new to me but I felt that I had come here on an errand of God and was ready for His disposal whatever it might be -- so I had little apprension.

> . . . The houses were so scattered as to make little impression and one would say 'where is the city'? . . . There was a small landing mole for passengers in the port, a fort on the point and cemetery nearby. . .there was little or no pavement, no gas or street lamps of any kind, no water supply save by carriers. The solitary street down to the Almendral* unsafe at night by reason of robbers from the *quebradas* (gullies).(1)

However dismal were the impressions of the location of the growing village, the spiritual wasteland of the English-speaking community was a matter of greater apprehension to the young minister. Again he wrote to his family,

> The ignorance here of the Gospel is painfully sinful and the American and English, many of them seem careless as to the why of things. I shall by God's grace begin to hold divine service on shore and hope to gather some of them to hear the truth and count of God's help to heed it. My part is to work then His is to give the increase.(2)

Notes in David Trumbull's Journals indicate that he made a good start in the fulfillment of his commission to seamen. On January 4, 1846 he wrote, "The first of this year my Bethel flag was hoisted on the *Mississippi* and an audience of some forty persons gathered to whom I preached on II Corinthians 4:4. . .for three months I have not failed to find some ship-master, pious, or at least well disposed, who has allowed the free use of his vessel for the service of God."

In his first report to the Seamen's Friend Society, cosponsor of the evangelist from New England, David wrote,

> This is the chief seaport of this coast. Last year, ending December 31st, 1845 about sixty-five American vessels entered. . . and about two hundred English. They were manned by upwards of 3,500 men probably, and how great the need, then, of Gospel truth being offered to them; even here where they have so often found the high road to ruin.(3)

In the beginning the Protestant Chaplain was restricted to holding religious services only on board the vessels in the harbor. Later however, having won the confidence and the support of the community and the permission of the civil authorities, he built a Sailor's Home and a Bethel Chapel on shore. Soon he was engaged in consoling the

---

* The *Almendral* was a section of the village, so called by the almond trees planted by the Agustine monks in that area in colonial days.

sick and lonely in the American and British hospitals and in visiting the foreign delinquents in the city prisons. (4)

The "grand errand" envisioned by David Trumbull was the establishment of the Reformed Church, first in Valparaiso, then in strategic locations throughout the nation. These were to be directed and supported by the people of the several communities. This was a daring adventure in view of the fact that the Organic Constitution of 1833 specifically stated that "the Roman Apostolic and Catholic Religion is and always will be the religion of the State to the exclusion of the public worship of all others."(5) Such a law proved to be contrary to the best interests of the developing nation, for it would have alienated sectors of society which were the source of trade, technical skills, industry and commerce. Much later, by way of an *Interpretative Act*, the right and privilege of worship for the non-Catholics was conceded.(6)

Following a period of celebrating worship in private homes, Union Church was organized by David Trumbull in 1847. The dissidents were not allowed to build a chapel for their services until 1855 and then only "if the building was behind a high board fence and without a steeple or bell."(7) It was twenty years before the Chilean congregation was organized and before permission was given to erect a building in the capital city for public worship. Such a building was dedicated with solemn ceremony and with great rejoicing on September 20, 1868. "Mr. José Manuel Ibañex Guzmán (1841-1875) delivered a spirited address to his countrymen composing the congregation."(8) In November of 1871, José Manuel Ibañez was ordained as the first Chilean, and in fact, the first Spanish-speaking Protestant minister in all America. The gifted and charming minister became a tower of strength and won the reputation of being the John Knox of the Chilean-Reformed Church.(9)

An out-post of the Valparaiso church was established at San Felipe, a village ninety miles to the north and the birthplace of Rev. José Manuel Ibañez. Robert McLean, a graduate of Auburn Seminary, was commissioned by the Presbyterian Mission Board to serve at this mission station. One of his first converts was a Spaniard by the name of Juan Bautista Canut. He in turn won so many converts that followers of the Evangelical faith were henceforth called, in derision, "Canutos".

To the south of Santiago, the capital, another mission outpost was established in 1869. This was at Talca, an important city in the central valley known for its viniculture. So great was the hostility and violence to the efforts to open a school and to organize a church that only the intervention of the governor of the province and the United States' Minister saved the Rev. Sylvanus Sayer and his wife from martyrdom.(10)

In response to David Trumbull's urgent request for superior reinforcements, "men who will be missed at home," the Presbyterian Mission Board sent to Chile in 1878 Eneas McLean, brother of Robert and also a graduate of Auburn Seminary.(11) He was sent to work in Concepción, third largest city in the nation and gateway to the provinces of the far south. With the cooperation of Juan B. Canut, visits were made to the surrounding villages and many friends were added to the church which was organized in 1880.

A strategic city in the far north of Chile was the booming mining town of Copiapó. The Rev. Samuel Julian Christen organized the Reformed Church here in 1873. He also founded an Academy in 1877 for meeting the educational needs of the boys of the members of a large foreign colony. It was called *Instituto Internacional* (International Institute). This school was moved to Santiago, the Capital, in 1884 and was known as *El Instituto Inglés* (English Institute) of the Chile Presbyterian Mission. From the beginning, in keeping with the Reformed tradition, schools were an important part of the "grand errand." David Trumbull and his colleagues established four such institutions to meet the needs and interests of the poor, the middle class and the elite. Across the years many thousands of Chilean youth were exposed to the Protestant ethic and the Anglo-Saxon ethos.(12)

With the gradual expansion of the Reformed Church there emerged a ground swell of public sentiment in its favor. The Catholic hierarchy was quite alarmed; prelates and curates pronounced anathemas and ex-communications in order to check the invasion of the "foreign heretics" and to confiscate their "fraudulent Bibles."(13) Commenting upon this stage of his apostolate, David Trumbull wrote:

> In Chile the path of entrance has been cut through the jungle, brushwood and undergrowth of popular opposition and legal prohibition, so that we have reached the open plains of free statement and discussion -- the Gospel has secured a hearing there; public men insist that the advocate of reformation in religion shall not be silenced by force, or by any legal obstruction. Our

opinions have already been cited on the floor and in the debates of the National congress of Chile, and we have only to go forward with the certainty, humanly speaking, that the Word of the Lord will grow and prevail there if disseminated *viva voce*, and on the printed page as it ought to be.(14)

A milestone in the development of the Chilean Reformed Church was the transfer in 1873 of the activities of the American and Foreign Christian Union to the Board of Missions of the Presbyterian Church in the U.S.A. This was due to a financial crisis of the Christian Union. David Trumbull repeatedly urged the Presbyterian Church to accept this responsibility, which it did, in spite of the fact that at that time the Board faced a debt of $128,000.(15)

Upon the arrival in 1883 of Rev. William H. Lester and William E. Dodge -- both reinforcements for the Misison from Auburn Seminary in New York, a Presbytery was organized.(16) This judicatory was incorporated into the General Assembly of the Presbyterian Church in the U.S.A. by way of enrollment in the Synod of New York. David Trumbull was reluctant to impose a denominational name on the Chilean Church but then he was assured by the Mission Board that it was not interested in Presbyterianizing the new adherents but only in evangelizing them with the expectation that they should soon become self-governing. (17)

In reference to the additional support of the emerging Presbyterian Church, the Board wrote:

> With the appointments made recently for the West Coast we think we have done pretty well. The only thing now will be to secure that strict economy of operations which bears ever in mind the fact that much of the money we remit is raised by poor people and in very small amounts. We do not sympathize with a great movement for theological education but believe that the shell should grow with the turtle, and not be first created as a magnificent structure with the key ready for the occupant. In this way a healthy religious work will be established, and one which the Chileans themselves will be able to carry forward largely on their own account in the future.(18)

The events of 1873 and 1884 were of far-reaching consequences. In 1964, having achieved self-support, the Chilean Church sought its juridical separation from the General Assembly of the United Presbyterian Church in the U.S.A. It then became associated with The Alliance of Reformed Churches Throughout the World Holding the Presbyterian Order.(19) By this act, the Chilean Reformed

Church became identified with the Christian Church of the sixteenth and the first centuries.

This brief story of the establishment of the Reformed Church in Chile covers a long period in the historical development of the nation. David Trumbull lived and labored, not without tears and toils and prayers, during the administration of seven presidents, from 1845-1889. The achievements during that lapse of time bordered upon the miraculous. It was a far cry from the time when the non-Catholics were obliged, by the law of the land, to worship secretly in an unadorned building behind a highboard fence to the day when the Reformed Church was established in strategic centers throughout the nation. He who tilled the soil and scattered the seed had every reason to believe, as the apostle did of old, that "the Lord added to their number day by day, those who were being saved (Acts 2:47).

6

AGENT OF THE EVANGELICAL MAGISTERIUM

Be ye transformed by the renewal of your mind (Romans 12:2)

A man of culture is he who understands the meaning of history, who appreciates the sacrifices involved in each new stage of knowledge; who accepts his share of responsibility in the particular social sphere in which he lives, be it in the family, profession or country. What this world needs more than informed men and technicians is better human quality, less selfishness, less useless pains, less exploitation of fellowmen, more compassion.

Amanda Labarca, Chilean Educator

The Philosophy of Education in the Reformed Tradition

In Geneva, Switzerland, stands a monument to John Calvin and his associates who initiated the Reformed Tradition. The group stands in front of an unfinished wall. The artistic motif gives expression to the continual renewal of the faith (*ecclesia reformata, sempre reformando*). The motto of classical Roman Catholicism is *Sempre Idem*; indicating the unchanging nature of the faith. No doubt these two expressions are complementary aspects of an ideology which would be mutually enriching if there could be a free and friendly confrontation.

In the Reformed Tradition high priority was given to the education of the populace, whereas in colonial Latin America education, by and large, has been limited to the elite and almost exclusively dominated by the Roman

Catholic Church. The founding fathers of Chile diligently advocated popular education. The Constitution of 1833 which was in effect until 1925, succinctly stated, "public education is the preferential obligation of the government."(1) When the University of Chile was founded in 1842 the statutes stated, "primary and secondary schools of the nation shall be under the direction of the University."(2) Don Manuel Montt, Minister of Education and later president of the Republic, was known as the patron of public education.

David Trumbull accepted the scriptural mandate "Go therefore and make disciples of all nations. . .teaching them to observe all that I have commanded you."(3) From 1851 to 1856, David and Jane Fitch Trumbull conducted the school for young ladies which was started by Isaac Wheelwright. Strenuous objections were made to this private non-Catholic school by the Church. It was denounced as a "center of corruption and immorality," and a commission was appointed to investigate it.

The report however was so favorable that "it gave an impetus to the school, at which many prominent ladies of this city were educated."(4) At this time of the nation's history only a few private schools were concerned with the education of women. These carried on in opposition by the Church. The private schools introduced progressive methods offering courses in liberal arts and sciences and stressing the formation of character and the democratic ideology. They opened the way for the Girls High Schools by the government. The first such High School was established in 1891 in Valparaiso by the Society of the Parents of Families. This school was later taken over by the Government and was called Liceo de Ninas Numero Uno de Valparaiso (Girls' High School Number One of Valparaiso).(5)

The Blas Cuevas School

In 1872 the Freemasons of the Chilean, French, German, English, and American Lodges founded a free elementary school for boys. It was called "The Blas Cuevas School" in honor of a philanthropist of that name. David Trumbull was for many years Deputy of the Grand Lodge of Massachusetts for the district of Chile. When he was president of the Board of Directors of this school an acrimonious controversy concerning the right to exist of this school arose and was ventilated in the most important newspapers of the nation. The ecclesiastical governor of Valparaiso accused the founders of this school of non-Catholic propaganda; that it was atheistic and was pernicious because it failed to teach religion as a basis for morality. In defence of the school, Dr. Ramon Allende Palidín wrote in the newspaper *La Patria*:

> The supporters of the school will in no case cease to do so nor renounce their duty to fight to death in the struggle between truth and error, between fanaticism and tolerance, between those who ask for light, freedom and justice in opposition to those who exploit conscience. We shall strive indefatigably and will never forsake the battle to break the worst tyranny of all -- that of the tyranny of conscience and thus clear the road of the barriers to widespread education of the masses and free them from the long yoke of colonialism.(6)

Other arguments in favor of the *Blas Cuevas School* held that the thousands of dissident foreigners and the freethinking Chileans could not be expected to have their children taught contrary to their own faith or unfaith. "Moral teaching" they said, "could be done without the indoctrination of sectarian dogma." It was not until 1865 by the *Interpretation Act* that dissidents were granted the right to teach their own faith and to be exempt from the religious examination for those who intended to pursue professional studies in the Universities.(7)

The Artizan School

In the year 1857 many circumstances conspired to make propitious the establishment of the Artizan School of Valparaiso. It was during the term of office of the liberal president Manuel Montt (1851-1861). The new nation was just beginning to exploit its abundant mineral resources. Railroads were being constructed and the Port city was a center of worldwide trade and ship servicing. Many families came from Scotland and England with technical skills in these enterprises, and industrial firms were being established to take advantage of the increasing opportunities in manufacturing, commerce and international trade.

The English language was becoming more and more the *lingua franca* of this west coast emporium. Bilingual and technically skilled personnel were needed for banking and commerce and for the construction and management of the communications media within the country and abroad. As the foreign population increased in Valparaiso it was natural that the concern for the vocational and moral education of the younger generation should be a real concern of the responsible leaders of the community. Rather than try to send children to the schools from whence their parents came, it would be much more viable to provide them the opportunity for education in the land of their adoption. All these circumstances gave rise to the formation of the

Aritzan School Society on January 5, 1857.(8) Its purpose was formulated as follows:

> The chief aim of the school is to afford the children of British and North American parents a solid English education, such as would be afforded in good schools at home. Other children are to be admitted as far as there is room.(9)

The issue of the teaching of religion gave rise to a serious controversy involving David Trumbull and prominent members of his church. Oswald Hardey Evans wrote:

> In the discussion of the curriculum of the school about to be founded, it was to be expected that the teaching of religion would have to be considered. Was the school to be denominational, or non-denominational -- that is to say, non-sectarian? The first was ruled out by the circumstances; children of Anglican parents had to be considered as well as those of sturdy Presbyterian views. Dr. Trumbull, moreover, was a Congregationalist. The question of the admission of children of Catholic parents does not appear to have been raised at an early date; that came later on. No doubt it was felt that the opposition of the clergy would effectively prevent Catholic parents from availing themselves of the benefits of the school. The cry of "proselytism" was bound to be raised -- and it was.
>
> A member of the community present at the general meeting, was so bold as to move that the school should be secular; but though this motion found a seconder, it was evidently frowned down, for nothing more was heard of it. In view of the strong religious convictions of Mr. Alexander Balfour and his partner, it was really a foregone conclusion that their views would prevail, for without their material support there was little likelihood of the school materializing.(10)

Mr. Alexander Balfour and his partner Stephen Williamson were co-founders of the prestigious mercantile firm Williamson-Balfour Company. The firm had made it a condition of the partnership that a fixed proportion of its profits was to be devoted to philanthropic purposes.(11) These founding members of the Artizan School Society insisted on the practice "that the days work should be invariably opened with a short Bible reading and repetition of the Lord's Prayer, conducted by the class master.(12) One of the teachers who professed to be agnostic refused to comply with this regulation which led to his dismissal. The case for the Committee of Management was stated as follows:

> A man who refuses to repeat the Lord's prayer can be no fitting teacher for my children. . . A letter was addressed to Mr. Balfour in England, and in due time it received a really formidable reply, signed by Messrs. Balfour and Williamson and

thirteen former residents of Valparaiso, including founders, members of the Society and Committee, and contributers to the school. One and all, it appears were animated by sincere zeal for religious teaching in the establishment, insisting that the opening with prayer and scripture-reading were not only essential, but the minimum...in any case it was a triumph for Dr. Trumbull and his supporters.(13)

The consequences of this "storm in a tea cup" led to the closing of the Artizan School in 1870. It was reorganized and reopened under the direction of the first Master, Mr. Peter Mackay. It became known as the English or Board School and later as The Mackay School. Peter Mackay was a close friend of David Trumbull and an active member of Union Church. Hardy Evans wrote of him:

Mr. Mackay held strong religious convictions which he shared with his friend Dr. David Trumbull, the American Pastor, though perhaps he did not follow him to extremes. Nevertheless, it is on record that these two zealots appealed to the management of the Pacific Steamship Company to give up sailings and other port activities of their vessels on the Sabbath.(14)

From 1857 to the reorganization of the Artizan School in the 1870's many distinguished young people were proud to call it their Alma Mater. Evans names the following:

Among them may be mentioned presidents Billinghurst and Ballivian, of Peru and Bolivia respectively, as well as, for a short time, Pierola, the famous revolutionist who made himself President of Peru, 1879. To the list may be added no less a name than that of Don Augusto Leguia, the famous and ill-fated President of Peru . . .Among Chileans of note Edward Delano and Agustin Edwards, father of Agustin Edwards who was for many years Chilean Minister and later Ambassador in Great Britain. Both Delano and Edwards became Cabinet Ministers; Alfred Delano, Richard Trumbull and John Craig became Deputies. Carlos Van Buren, grandson of President Van Buren of the United States, a philanthropist and benefactor to Valparaiso, was a boarder at Los Olivos and received his education entirely in the school. . . There is some evidence that Don Jose Toribio Medina, the famous Latin American bibliographer, studied English in the Valparaiso "board school."(15)

At each class reunion these graduates rendered tribute to the stern Anglo-Saxon discipline and the exemplary christian virtues of their teachers. The underlying principles and ideals of the Artizan School are fittingly expressed in its shield; a cross encircled by a crown -- and below the motto *Vincit Qui Se Vincit* (He conquers who conquers himself). A Chilean historian evaluates this Evangelical Magisterium in the following passage.

A secondary school which met a real need in the third quarter of the XIX century was the Mackay School of Valparaiso. Peter Mackay, its founder arrived at Valparaiso October 8, 1857. He adopted a curriculum as conceived by the English, designed for the formation of character, striving for a sane balance, coordinating the native culture with the trends of modern society and based upon the work of a free man and not upon the arm of the slave nor the praise of the vassal.(16)

La Escuela Popular (A School for the People)

In Valparaiso, Chile, a school still operates which was established in July of 1869 by David Trumbull and his colleague Alexander M. Merwin. For many years it was called *La Escuela Popular* (School for the People) but recently the name has been changed to *Colegio David Trumbull*. This change was made in grateful memory of the subject of this biographical narrative who, following the Reformed tradition, gave high priority to the educational ministry. The purpose of the school was recorded as follows:

> Its first purpose was to afford a primary education to children of Protestant Chileans who objected to the religious errors taught in the public schools of the city. Not only was the Roman catechism taught there, but the children were subject to personal annoyance as "heretics-Jews-Masons-infidels" -- epithets that often were hurled at them.
>
> The Holy Scriptures are exalted to the place of honor in the school and the holy commandments are taught as the divine word of life.
>
> In past years the clergy made strenuous opposition to the school, railing against it from the pulpit and seeking to induce the authorities to close its doors. They succeeded regarding another school in the *Almendra*, but this one outlived their punny assaults, and has until this day held its own; winning the confidence of parents, the love of the children and sympathy of outsiders, it has gone on gaining year after year a higher position and achieving greater success.(17)

The success has been considerable. For more than a century now, thousands of boys and girls were exposed to the progressive methods of this model school of integral education. The main school set the pattern for others in the suburbs and in schools annexed to the evangelical churches in other parts of the country.

These *Escuelas Populares* met a felt need of the nation. They helped make more effective the Law of Obligatory

Elementary Education of 1860. They contributed to the formation of the middle class. They provided bilingual junior clerks for the several foreign banks in the Port city. They became centers of cultural interchange between South and North America. The names of many teachers from the United States became household words for a host of Chilean boys and girls.

The *Escuelas Populares* enjoyed the favor of public administrators. One such director said "The Escuela Popular has achieved a certain *mystique* which makes it a unique center of learning."(18) For the celebration of the 70th anniversary of *El Colegio David Trumbull* the youngest daughter of the co-founder wrote:

> It is a great pleasure to express my deep appreciation for the splendid work of the sincere christian workers in the *Escuela Popular* during these many years. I remember with great pleasure the first few days of its establishment. Mr. Merwin, with his consecrated endeavors, Mrs. Betty, so kind who gave so much of her strength, teaching principles of self-support and classes of sewing.
>
> My brother, William Trumbull, was in charge of the school for a year (I think it was in 1886). I remember that I had a class for the youngest children on Friday afternoons, telling stories and teaching them Bible truths; how happy they made me with their great interest in listening to me.
>
> May God give to Chile many other *Escuelas Populares* in order to multiply the good work begun seventy years ago.
>
> > Julia Trumbull Dodge,
> > Altadena, California
> > October 13, 1938 (19)

The Instituto Inglés (English Academy)

As was mentioned in Chapter V the *Instituto Internacional* (International Institute) was established in 1877 under the auspices of the Reformed Church in the northern city of Copiapó. When it was moved to the capital city of Santiago, its name was changed to *Institute Inglés* (English Academy). The original design was to make it "The Robert College of the Pacific Coast." For more than seventy-five years it became a center of co-mingling of the Chilean culture with that of North America. It was the forerunner of the many bi-cultural institutes which later became popular in several other Latin America countries.

The curriculum in the early days provided academic training for the candidates for the evangelical ministry. For the general public, besides courses in English and Commercial disciplines, much importance was given to the formation of character based upon a non-sectarian teaching of the christian faith. In that the school met the needs and aspirations of people in the local community and also served the purposes of the national government. The *Instituto Inglés* was highly esteemed. Its graduates were accepted as candidates for the professional studies in the State University. The alumni were to be found in practically all the important positions in the communities of the Republic. At the portal of the main building of its spacious campus are the words "Enter to Learn -- Go Forth to Serve." On the emblem of the school are the words "Truth-Honor-Power." The *Instituto* was granted the special concession by the government to demonstrate the advantages of the North American Dalton System of Education. This was designed to develop individual initiative and personal responsibility. It also served as a model for other Experimental Schools under the direction of the Educational Administration of the government.

After eighty years of distinguished service to Chile, and believing that the *Instituto Inglés* had accomplished its original goals, it turned over its twelve-acre campus and mission-style buildings (at a nominal price) to the Chilean government. It now serves as the Normal School Department of the State University. However indirect was its approach to the propagation of the Gospel this school, as well as the others sponsored by David Trumbull, created a climate of appreciation and acceptance of the Evangelical ideology.(20)

7

THE WORD OF GOD IS SPREAD ABROAD

So shall my word be that goeth forth out of my mouth; it shall not return unto me void but it shall accomplish that which I please, and it shall prosper in the thing whereto I sent it.
(Isaiah 55:11)

For ye shall go out with joy, and be led forth with peace; the mountains and the hills shall break forth before you into singing, and all the trees of the field shall clap their hands.
(Isaish 55:11-12)

. . . for the earth shall be full of the knowledge of the Lord, as the waters cover the sea.
(Isaish 11:9)

Biblical faith envisioned the welfare and destiny of the nations as determined by the will and the Word of God. This was the faith and counsel of forerunner Rev. John C. Brigham, pioneer agent of the American Board of Commissioners for Foreign Missions and long-time secretary of the American Bible Society. In 1826 he reported to the American Board and the American Bible Society that the Bible was practically an unknown book in Latin America, and that the enlightenment and the development of the new republics was contingent upon a wide diffusion of the Scriptures. He recommended that Valparaiso, Chile should be the location of one of such depositories to serve this purpose.

In response to this urgent plea the Rev. Isaac Wheelwright was appointed in 1833 as the first resident agent on the Pacific Coast of South America of the American Bible Society. So much opposition was made to this agency that it was closed in 1837.(1) On March 12, 1858, Archbishop Rafael Valentin Valdivieso of Santiago, Chile, directed a formidable Pastoral letter to the "Clergy and Faithful" of his archdiocese menacing with the severest penalties of the Church all those who should depart from her teachings, and saying:

> The chief means which the Protestants employ in their anti-Catholic propaganda is the distribution of fradulent Bibles and tracts written from a Protestant viewpoint, and with calculated malice to deceive the ignorant, which the so-called Bible Societies print in unheard of profusion for circulation in countries where our language is spoken, through agents abundantly remunerated with the money of their numerous associates.(2)

In answer to such a serious charge David Trumbull carried on a public debate with Presbyter Francisco Martínez Garfías, representing the Archbishop. This debate was published and widely distributed. It bore the title, "Vindication of the Various Versions of the Bible, published by the Bible Societies, Against the Imputations of Presbyter Francisco Martinez Garfías." The Dedication of this pamphlet reveals some of the basic issues at stake:

> This republication of the letters to Mr. Martinez with mine, is dedicated to the inhabitants of Chile, and the other Spanish republics. The Bible Societies claim that the original documents concerning the Christian religion should be universally read and observed as the supreme authority, to which criterion every opinion should be submitted.
>
> For these countries there have been published various editions of the Holy Scriptures, both with and without the apocryphal books. God has given this precious gift to all nations. Since the Reformation we have proved its beneficial influence on us, and we earnestly desire that it may impart its light to all. Knowing that religion ought not to be neglected, we advise everyone to inform himself personally as to what God has revealed. Jesus Christ, than whom a higher authority does not exist on earth has said 'Search the Scriptures'.
>
> This is our position, and this we recommend to all. It is right to investigate -- it is not right to seek a monopoly. Those times have passed away. They belong to the epoch of the inquisition, and of sentences read on the scaffold (de los autos de fe). But now the laymen, as well as the clergy, enjoy the privilege, and are under obligation to listen to the doctrines as they come from the inspired books. Here is the foundation stone upon which the Reformation rests.(3)

The Word of God is Spread Abroad 77

The debate concerning the "fradulent Bibles" resulted in the opposite effect from that intended by the overzealous prelate. It did more for the distribution of the prohibited Book than the dissemination of many paid agents. The Spanish translations of the Scriptures by Casidor de Reina in 1569, and revised by Cipriano de Valera in 1602 proved to be more in accord with the original Hebrew and Greek texts, than were the Spanish translations of Felipe Scio de San Miguel in 1793 and that of Felix Torres Amat in 1823, the latter two having been translations of the Vulgate or Latin text of Jerome in A.D. 388.

The public debate also served to inform multitudes of some essential differences between the two branches of the Christian Church. The Anglo-Saxon fair-mindedness combined with a certain Latin-American courtesy, which characterized polemicist David Trumbull, won many adherents to the tenets of the Reformation.

The controversy concerning the authenticity of the translation of the Scriptures was based on the pronouncements of the Council of Trent (1545-1560):

> The doctrinal decrees of the Council of Trent were clear and definite in their rejection of Protestant beliefs, while often indecisive regarding matters of dispute in mediaeval controversies. Scripture and tradition are equally sources of truth. The Church alone has the right of interpretation. Justification is skillfully defined, yet so as to leave scope for work-merit. The sacraments are the mediaeval seven and defined in the mediaeval way. The result is ably expressed but the church had shut the door completely to all compromise or modification of the mediaeval doctrine.(4)

The Council had also declared that the Vulgate was the only acceptable text and that the Apocryphal books were to be considered as canonical. No translations were approved which did not include additional notes which interpreted the Scriptures in accordance with the dogmas and doctrines of the Roman Catholic Church. Pope Leo XII (1823-1829) and Pius IX (1846-1878) condemned the translations of the Bible Societies, repudiated the toleration of varieties in religion, the separation of Church and State and modernism.(5)

The Reformation leaders in turn, guided by the principle of *Sola Scriptura*, repudiated dogmas and doctrines of the Catholic tradition which were not found in the canonical Scriptures. They also justified the translation of the original texts of the Scriptures in the language of the common people in keeping with the rationale for the Vulgate version.

The Bible Societies were established so that the Word of God should be known to all peoples everywhere. They were willing to provide copies of the Scriptures based on the Vulgate texts, including the Apocryphal books plus Catholic notes -- this in spite of the prefered rule of printing and distributing editions without notes. Given the traditional restrictions concerning the translation and distribution of the Scriptures on the part of the Roman Catholic Church and given the reports of the agents of the Reformation to the effect that the Bible in Chile was an "unknown-book," the extraordinary story of the Vaughan publication and distribution of a revised edition of the Scio translation of the New Testament is of cogent relevance to the issues involved in this historical controversy.

In 1872 Jesuit Father Kenelm Vaughn, brother of Cardinal Herbert Vaughn of England, visited Latin America. He was abashed to note the religious scepticism and relaxed moral conditions in the several republics. In order to counteract these lamentable realities he advocated a wide distribution of the Scriptures. His declaration of war against such enemies was published in The South Pacific Times as follows:

> Sir: I am planning a war -- a holy war, a just war and a necessary war. And I call upon all lovers and defenders of liberty, truth, and intellectual progress to give me their co-operation and alliance. This war is not against flesh and blood, but against the intellectual immoralities of the age. It is directed not against the agressors of the body, but those of men's higher and superior nature -- his intelligence. At the head of these adversaries of progressive thought and enlightment rides Infidelity. Positivism, originated by Comte -- is leading many thousands of young men of the age from their allegience to Revelation, and subjecting them ignominiously to what is really nothing less than rank atheism. . .Ignorance, superstition, sorcery, fanaticism and formalism are assuming despotism over humbler classes, keeping them bound in barbarous mental servitude.
>
> But there is one weapon which excells them all in power and efficiency -- sanctioned and especially prescribed by the Church -- not carnal but spiritual. This weapon is the *Holy Scripture*, the Divine instrument I wish to introduce into the field of combat. To enable me to put every man, woman and child in possession of this instrument of war, I propose to begin by stereotyping the New Testament.
>
> Yours faithfully,
> Kenelm Vaughan,
> Chaplain's House, Bethlehem College
> (6)

The Word of God is Spread Abroad

This unique enterprise was readily supported by Catholics and Protestants. David Trumbull raised thousands of dollars for the project. An edition of 140,000 of the Vaughan New Testaments was printed in London in 1874. It bore the *Nihil obstat* of Fr. Ligorius M. Echevarria and the *Imprimatur* of Henricus Edwardus, *Archiepiscopus Westmonasteriensis*. It also bore a Decree of the Archbishop of Santiago, Chile, December 26, 1872, approving the notes of this edition, and a letter from Pope Pius VI of April, 1778, recommending to the faithful the reading of Scriptures as translated from the Vulgate and accompanied with notes.(7)

Unfortunately only a few of the 14,000 Vaughan New Testaments intended for the distribution in Chile were circulated. For some unknown reason the shipment from London to Chile was lost in Panama and was not found until 1876. In March of 1880 it was reported from Chile that "there are thousands of Father Vaughan's New Testaments securely boxed, in a warehouse here, but not a single copy to be found in any shop window of these crowded streets." Finally, Father Vaughan, returning to Chile in June of 1900, reported that "he had found the storehouse in Valparaiso, Chile where the Testaments known as the 'Vaughan' had been sleeping between 25 and 30 years, and that he was now occupied with their distribution and usefulness."(8)

In 1877, David Trumbull wrote in *The Record:*

> ... the translation is not all that could be desired. It is in effect a Spanish translation of the Vulgate and the Douay Bible. Not only are those gross inaccuracies reproduced which disfigure the text of the English Roman Catholic Bible, but the "Index of Proof Texts" at the end of the volumes, undertakes to give passages in support of many of the erroneous doctrines of Rome. In spite of this however, it is a proper subject, for rejoicing that even so imperfect a copy of God's Word is now offered in the name of the Roman Church. We may well hope that it will enter homes where the more correct text offered by our Protestant missionaries could not obtain a welcome.(9)

In this same issue of *The Record*, David Trumbull reported concerning the burning of Bibles and religious books at Tongoi, in the north of Chile. This event followed one of the Missions which were sometimes designed to stir up the faithful against the Protestant heretics.

The Establishment of the Valparaiso Bible Society

From the foregoing episode it would seem that the Roman Catholic Church in Chile was not disposed to encourage the reading of the Scriptures even though their own versions with notes were distributed. The thousands of Bibles distributed by James Thompson for use in the Lancastrian Schools were not to be found. From the founding of the Chilean Republic there was a pattern of prohibition of the reading and distribution of the Scriptures printed by the Bible Societies. On the other hand the agents of the Reformed Church were persuaded that the Bible contained the answers to the needs and aspirations of peoples and their societies and that they were called of God to spread abroad the textbook of the human race. Forerunners of David Trumbull had said that the time was "not yet" for the direct preaching of the Gospel but that the distribution of the Scriptures would open the way for the spoken Word of God. Given these antecedents, the Bible Society of Valparaiso, Chile, was established in 1861, independent of, but supported by funds and Scriptures from the British and Foreign Gospel Society, the American Bible Society, The National Bible Society of Scotland, The American Tract Society of London and New York, and the Seamen's Friend Society of New York. All these agencies were committed to the cause of creating the Great Society of the Kingdom of God on the Southern Continent. A host of individual supporters should be remembered, especially the co-founder of the Valparaiso Bible Society, namely, Alexander Balfour, a Christian business man and long-time friend of David Trumbull, who, with his business partner Steven Williamson, contributed so generously to the schools, hospitals, churches, and Seminaries of their adopted country. In the history of this business firm we read:

> Trumbull, a clergyman of the Congregational Church in America, with a congregation in Valparaiso predominatly Scottish Presbyterian, was almost entirely financed by the firm. He had a large family and a most generous nature. Though careless of personal comfort, he was usually in need of money. The Firm, under Alexander's leadership, made it their special responsibility to see that he was properly provided for. They guaranteed most of his salary, liquidated the debt on his house and paid for his holidays and medical expenses. . . Closely associated with the Union Church was the Valparaiso Bible Society, founded in 1861 for the sale of Bibles and other religious books in all languages. It was in touch with similar organizations in Britain and America.
>
> In 1862 the Society opened a shop on one of Valparaiso's main streets. A German colporteur was engaged to run the shop and to visit the ships at anchor in the bay, the English, French and Chilean hospitals, and people's homes. He was a wonderful success. 'There is a great demand for religious books in Spanish' wrote Mrs. Williamson, 'and many copies of the Dairyman's Daughter, Pilgrim's Progress and etc. have been sold. This shop is a new

The Word of God is Spread Abroad 81

>idea originated by Mr. Balfour, Dr. Trumbull and Steven and others who take interest in what is good. Every day now the colporteur is selling Bibles and good books to natives and foreigners.(10)

David Trumbull was president of the Valparaiso Bible Society for many years. For forty years he was a regular correspondent of British and Foreign and the American Bible Societies, but never was he a paid agent of the same. Excerpts from his Annual Reports reveal how convinced he was that the Bible was indispensable, the enhancement of every man and the promise of peace and progress of Chile. They also indicate the wide frontier of his passionate concern and the amazing statistics of the distribution of the Bible and religious literature in spite of persecutions and persistent efforts to restrict the Protestant "propaganda"; from the Annual Report of 1879 we read:

> The west coast of South America is not a small field. We ourselves cannot venture to look beyond Chile but in the north of Chile to Panama there are some five millions of people who have no access to the Word of God and it is a little credit to the Christian enterprise that nothing is done to remedy this want.
>
> The political and social benefits which would be gained from a frank and honest acceptance of the Bible as a basis of guidance, are obviously so great that were it nothing else, it would be the duty of all friends of human progress, to keep it in view of the people of Chile, while those who have the happiness to know from their own experience, what the elevating power of the Holy Spirit is and what its individual benefit -- would fail of charity to their neighbors did they not press it on the attention of all, under whose notice they succeed in bringing it. We do not imagine, however, that the mere presentation of the Bible will restore a disorganized family nor the distribution of a thousand, or ten thousand copies of the Scriptures, reform the morals of a nation. The presentation of the volume is the only means toward ends so desirable.(11)

From the Annual Report of the Valparaiso Bible Society for 1884 we read:

> Public opinion among the natives has, ever since I knew Chile, insisted that those who desired to circulate the Holy Scriptures in Spanish should enjoy unfettered freedom and, so far as the Government was concerned, be unhindered. The only difficulty we have to contend with, the only obstacle to surmount that really taxes our skill and energy now, is the opposition, conscientious if you please, but thoroughly mistaken, of the Dominant, the Established Church, which bids the people not to read that which more than all else they need to read, i. e. the revealed Word of the Infinite and Eternal God. . . .As a Society we make nothing, we gain no profits. We ask none, we bear loss pecuniarly, but we

are resolute and determined to do what we can for the emancipation of the people of Chile from the religious servitude under which they have hitherto been detained.(12)

From the Annual Report for 1886 of the Valparaiso Bible Society we learn that four colporteurs were employed, not only to distribute the Scriptures and religious literature in Chile, but also in the neighboring Republics. Andres M. Milne, Continental Agent for the Bible Societies from 1864 to 1907, reported that he found books from the Valparaiso depository in Colombia, Ecuador, Peru, and Bolivia. The chairman of the Society reported that "more than ever before, the people of this country, (Chile) express a willingness to purchase and to read the Holy Scriptures. In Chile," he said, "a Bible from this Society moved a whole neighborhood, and again, men in factories and on trains were willing to buy the Word of God."(13) One of the colporteurs reported:

> In the port of Taltal (northern Chile) I met with a man named Quiroga, who had been truly converted by the simple reading of a New Testament. Strange to say, the book was dug from the ruins of a house which had been destroyed by a tidal wave.(14)

No doubt the New Testament which Juan Canut de Bon found in a trash-container in the railroad station at Quillota, Chile, was also distributed from the Valparaiso Bible Society's depository.

From the Seventy-third Report of the American Bible Society we are informed that during the twenty-seven years of its operation, the Valparaiso Bible Society distributed 54,417 copies of the Scriptures.(15) In 1910 the total number was 123,670.(16)

In 1905 the Valparaiso Bible Society became a regular auxiliary of the British and Foreign Bible Society. The secretary was appointed as an agent for the whole of the West Coast of South America. In 1946 the British and American Bible Societies formed a joint agency. The report from Chile of the United Bible Societies of January 1968 gives the following information:

> The Protestant churches of Chile, representing an 11% minority of the population, are making increasing use of the Scriptures in their outreach. This is apparent from the Bible Society's distribution figures for 1967, which showed a 130% increase over the previous year. Two and a quarter million Scriptures were distributed. Not only were small portions and selections of the Bible widely distributed in evangelistic efforts, but sales of complete Bibles and New Testaments have increased, suggesting that distribution of portions in the past has led to greater demand for the complete Book.(14)

The Word of God is Spread Abroad

There is hardly a village in Chile today which does not have an evangelical sanctuary even though it may be a single room of a home set apart for corporate worship. Native leadership has become a characteristic mark of this rapidly growing spiritual and moral movement which owes so much to the pioneer leader David Trumbull and to Union Church of Valparaiso, Chile. The widespread distribution of the Scriptures was interpreted by its agents to be the fulfillment of the prophetic promise,

> . . .ye shall go out with joy, and be led forth with peace; and the mountains and the hills shall break forth before you into singing. . .for the earth shall be full of the knowledge of the Lord, as the waters cover the sea.
>
> (Isaish 55:11; 11:9)

JOSE MANUEL IBAÑEZ GUZMAN (1841-1875)
A protegé of David Trumbull, he was the first Spanish-speaking Protestant minister in Latin America, ordained in 1871.

MEMBERS OF THE CHILEAN PRESBYTERY IN THE 1880's
Back row, left to right: Rev. Samuel J. Christen, D.D., Elder Nathaniel Bercovitz, Rev. Albert J. Vidaurre, Elder Aberlado Daroch, Elder Juan Bahamondes, Rev. James F. Garvin

Front row, left to right: Rev. W. H. Lester, D.D., Rev. W. E. Dodge, Rev. J. M. Allis, D.D., Rev. Francisco Jorquera, Rev. William B. Boomer

THE PRESBYTERIAN MISSION OF CHILE, JANUARY 1932

From five missionaries in 1873, the Chilean Presbyterian Mission grew to its greatest number of twenty-six members in 1932. From its beginning it worked in cooperation with the Chilean Presbytery and was integrated with the Chilean Presbyterian Church in 1964.

8

THE GOSPEL IN THE REFORMED TRADITION

*Man's chief end is to glorify God, and to enjoy Him forever.
(Shorter Catechism of the Westminster Confession of Faith)*

What was the Gospel that David Trumbull preached and practiced which brought about so great a change from original rejection to ultimate tolerance of the Reformed Tradition in Chile? No doubt the theological education which he received at liberal Yale College and orthodox Princeton Seminary enabled him to be an effective polemicist in the confrontation of two ideologies which were so different in matters of race, religion, and life-style. The establishment of Union Church in Valparaiso and other Reformed Churches in strategic communities of the Republic, the exposure of thousands of Chilean youth to Christian discipline in the schools sponsored by David Trumbull, the wide distribution of the Scriptures in the face of strenuous opposition -- all these were milestones in the fulfillment of the goals of the evangelist from Connecticut.

There is no simple answer to what in fact was the Gospel message, in that the multiple forces which bear upon people and their cultures are so complex that simple answers are prone to be wrong. However, some basic beliefs and practices which have a long tradition may be identified as characteristic of the Evangelical and Reformed ideology in contrast to different ways of faith and practice. Fortunately, primary sources are available for research in the life and thought of David Trumbull. From 1871 to 1889 he published a biweekly periodical called *The Record*. This was supported by voluntary

The Gospel in the Reformed Tradition

contributions and was widely distributed in Chile and in neighboring countries. Hardly an issue appeared which did not publish a sermon by the pioneer missionary. These were often translated into Spanish and published in the periodical *El Predicador* (The Preacher). In addition to the sermons, the *Record* published national and foreign news items and thus met the needs of those of the English-speaking community who did not read the newspapers in Spanish.

A survey of these many sermons and discourses delivered by David Trumbull helps the reader to identify some basic tenets of the Reformed Tradition. These reflect quite consistently the Calvinistic thinking which conditioned the life and thought of the Reformed Church on the continent of Europe and the Puritan cultures of England and New England. The sermons were methodically an exposition of a Biblical text. The presentation and interpretation proceeded in three or four sections and always ended with a practical application to contemporary life. Close reasoning, often involving the translation of words from Hebrew, Greek, Latin, and Sanskrit, were combined with timely illustrations. In this chapter, a brief statement is made of some of the doctrines which characterize the Gospel according to the Reformed Tradition.

First of all there is to be noted a profound conviction and utter faith in the Sovereign Majesty and Grace of the Triune God. He is Creator, Sustainer, Redeemer and Judge of all of life. His Providence rules over all. His purpose and ways are manifest in the ever-unfolding events which are perceived as Salvation-History. God is a Covenant God who chose a people and a church to serve as agents and witnesses of the Good News of His judgement and redeeming love in all ages and on all frontiers of the world. In a word, as was noted in the call and education of David Trumbull, he could say that he was:

> . . . a servant of God and apostle of Jesus Christ, to further the faith of God's elect and their knowledge of the truth which accords with godliness in hope of eternal life which God, who never lies, promised ages ago and at the proper time manifested in his word through the preaching with which I have been entrusted by command of God our Savior.
>
> (Titus 1:1)

This message was truly *Good News* to many a spiritual orphan in Chile who, while wistfully longing for a satisfying way of life, scoffed at the very idea of the existence of God.

The Splendor and Tragedy of Man

We read in the Scriptures that man was made in the image of God and was appointed to "have dominion...over every living thing that moveth upon the earth" (Genesis I: 27-28). We read in the Westminster Confession of Faith (in answer to the question of the Catechism), "The Chief end of man is to glorify God and to enjoy Him forever." These are positive aspects of man's destiny and the wellspring of his splendor. Orthodox Calvinists are sometimes decried because they stress the negative doctrines of man's total depravity and the eternal reprobation of the non-elect.

In the following excerpts of the sermons of David Trumbull there is a felicitous resolution of the false diochotomy of *either-or*. Without denying negative realities, the positive factors are stressed. This interpretive principle holds polar opposites in creative tension and thus transmuts discord into concord. In the sermon preached at Union Church in Valparaiso on September 7, 1884, the text was:

> Therefore being justified by faith we have peace with God through our Lord Jesus Christ (Romans 5:1).

In the exposition of this text the depravity of man is not explained in terms of the imputation of original sin but in terms of moral responsibility of the individual.

> Friends object to the word *depravity*, but as a matter of fact, do men commonly incline toward God? Do statistics show that they seek Him and remember His law and keep it? They who do are not depraved; but they who do not are. If any are self-indulgent, careless, ready when interest serves or pleasure to disregard God's laws, they are depraved. The word may have unpleasant associations, but it has a true significance...the word means turned down, away from God, adverse to Him, and inclined to less worthy objects of fear or love; love of self, promotion, indulgence, wicked gain; fear of men's scorn, pecuniary loss, or the yoke of Christian tasks -- in any event the soul is disinclined to its Maker's claims and does not hearken to Him.

In this simple every day language, David Trumbull interprets the traditional doctrines of man's imperfections and his alienation from his Maker. He was too familiar with sin and guilt and demonic forces not to recognize fully man's predicament and his need for redemption.

The sermon text for June 12, 1887 was:

> And hope maketh not ashamed, because the love of God is shed abroad in our hearts by the Holy Ghost which is given unto us (Romans 5:5).

The Gospel in the Reformed Tradition

In David Trumbull's interpretation of this text one notes again the application of the integral principle of *both-and* in preference to the principle of *either-or*; man co-operates with the Holy Spirit to achieve his salvation. Such dual action is quite in accord with the Biblical injunction. . .work out your own salvation with fear and trembling; for it is God which worketh in you both to will and to do his good pleasure (Philippians 2:12-13). The exposition was as follows:

> Here is a *catena*, a chain of several links, grace, tribulation, patience, experience and hope, the last of which takes a direct hold on things invisible but eternal, on present godliness and celestial advancement. Hope is linked with experience, probation, trial, that which tests character. There is only one way to produce veterans and that is by conflict. As this makes the recruit reliable, stalwart, courageous, and hence successful, so in the same way the believer obtains stamina and firmness by being tested, tried and subjected to the burdens of military duty, in the church and in the world, under the captain of his salvation.
>
> Now the hope that grows out of such experimental piety, out of conviction of sin in us, of Righteousness in God and of Judgment to come, 'Maketh not ashamed' or, as the Revised Version gives the phrase, 'putteth not to shame'. One who has asked for the Holy Spirit to influence his mental powers in the seats of emotions and spiritual life, and into whose heart the Spirit has been shed abroad in reply, cannot fail to take a grand estimate of the Grace of God.

In a word, this is what the apostle Paul was saying in the text:

> . . .work out your own salvation with fear and trembling; for it is God which worketh in you both to will and to do his good pleasure (Philippians 2:12-13).

John Calvin would have said "Work as though your salvation depended upon your own merits but pray as though everything depended upon the Grace of God." This interpretation is in accord with his saying, "we are justified, not without works, yet not by works."(1) The Gospel in the Reformed Tradition as interpreted by David Trumbull in these two brief excerpts from his sermons, holds in creative tension the apparent ambiguities of determinism and freedom, reason and revelation, faith and works, individual piety and social concern, the Law and the Gospels, the sovereignty of God and the free will and moral responsibility of man. The Peace of God which comes by faith in Jesus Christ brings hope to frustrated man enslaved as he finds himself to sin, and guilt, and the multiple burdens of his misery arising from fears and anxieties and exploitations of his fellowmen. Peace with God and hope certainly are Good News to those who were once:

> separated from Christ, alienated from the commonwealth of Israel, and strangers to the covenants of promise, having no hope and without God in the world (Ephesians 2:12).

The sermon on "Peace with God through our Lord Jesus Christ" (Romans 5:1) was translated into Spanish and printed in the periodical El Predicador (The Preacher). Twenty-five hundred copies of this number were put into circulation.(2)

Jesus Christ, Son of God, Savior

In the sermons cited above it is worthy of note that peace, hope and grace are contingent upon faith in Jesus Christ. Another characteristic of David Trumbull's sermons was his predilection for the interpretation of the Gospel in terms of Pauline theology. He agrees fully with Paul's simple yet profound creed that:

> if you confess with your lips that Jesus is Lord, and believe in your heart that God raised him from the dead, you will be saved (Romans 10:9).

The Scriptures for David Trumbull were the written Word of God, but Jesus Christ was the Living Word and the core of the Gospel message. This Christo-centric faith is succinctly expressed in the discourse of David Trumbull at the opening of the Annual Meeting of the Valparaiso Bible Society:

> ....the Savior is the crown of the Bible, its outcome, its flower. The Bible is the word of God and He too is the Word in wonderous personalism. Human knowledge in its advance and retrogression, in its achievements and errors, raises questions multiform of history, ethnology, astronomy and geology; questions which as yet have been insufficiently answered; but the Redeemer reveals the face of a loving God to whom the anxious, however unlearned, may appeal, and in whom learn to trust with results at once peaceful and satisfying. He teaches the doctrine of universal charity, of love to men because of love of God, of love to God because He hath first loved us. No man ever learned of Christ without being enobled. If His disciples have been faulty, the fault has not been in His instruction nor in His example, but in some failure on their part to understand or to follow Him.(3)

The Rev. W. E. Dodge, associate pastor and son-in-law of
David Trumbull, wrote of the centrality of Jesus Christ as
the Savior of the world in the thought and life of his
colleague;

> As a theologian, Dr. Trumbull was too thorough and skillful to
> accept anything short of conclusions which embraced satisfactorily
> all the conditions and phases of given questions. He looked too
> deeply into the problem of human life to apologize for sin. He
> knew that God should be honored by a true obedience, and the sac-
> rifice of Christ was to him a real atonement.
>
> David Trumbull felt personally the power of Him whose touch
> opened the eyes of the blind; Jesus was and so he preached Christ
> and Him crucified, and pure unchanged Gospel that this poor world
> needs. Would you know the source of his strength, the power that
> moulded that consecrated life -- behold it in Jesus Christ up-
> lifted!
>
> He loved his Saviour, he lived to honor God, and this is the true
> explanation of the religious heroism, of the good fight of faith,
> of the patriotic noble, lovable, sympathizing character, to which
> so many render sincere homage this day.(4)

David Trumbull had homiletic skill to interpret the new
life in the risen Lord in terms of simple everyday experiences. The following excerpt as recorded in his Class
Letter to Yale University in 1888 is a case in point. He
is illustrating the quickening of the soul to spiritual
life as based on the text: I came that they might have
life, and have it more abundantly (John 10:10).

> Some years ago a lad in my native town, a schoolmate of mine, was
> riding on horseback. The steed was spirited, became unmanageable
> and ran away. The lad kept on as long as he could, but finally
> fell, or was thrown, and was dragged with a foot in the stirrup,
> along the road until, his shoe coming off, he was picked up and
> carried into the nearest house. It was my father's house; and
> the anxious question arose did life remain in the youth or was it
> extinct. His family sent for medical aid was procured. Various
> things were applied, and all watched in suspense for the slight-
> est token of returning vitality. But there was no such token.
> All was in vain. Life had fled. His remains were taken home,
> and soon after we who had been at school with him the day of the
> accident, were called to join his friends as his body was laid in
> the ground.
>
> Not long after that, that is to say, not many months a similar
> accident occured. Another lad was dragged in the very same way,
> and was brought into the same identical dwelling, apparently as
> lifeless as the other had proved to be. It was not only my home,
> but it was my own life that seemed then to have fled. For me to

recount what was said and done, is impossible. You must imagine how the family felt after that earlier experience. But I was afterwards told how my parents, who had cared for their neighbor's boy under circumstances so identical and with results so fatal, looked most anxiously for an hour for the last symptom or sigh of life, all the while perceiving none. They had, however sent to town for the family physician, and his more practiced eye and touch gave them an encouraging shade of hope. Till then I knew absolutely nothing, being entirely unconscious; but even now at this distance of time can recall with vividness how at the prick of a lancet my sense returned and I heard the rejoicing of many around that really the life was restored. Let us now illustrate the value of life, for something like it Jesus would have every soul experience who is here today, if not already alive unto God. For all who are paralyzed, stunned, dead in trespasses and sins, He came that they might have life! He waits to give it. Waits for each one to ask for it and consent to accept it at His hands.

For David Trumbull, as for the apostle Paul, "God was in Christ reconciling the world to himself." The disciples of Christ are, "ambassadors to whom is given the ministry of reconciliation" (II Corinthians 5:19-20). This was good news to those who were lost in a thousand and one ways in the quest for the abundant life, especially at a time when a society was in the throes of socio-economic and political instability. It was good news to and for such people to know that Jesus Christ was the answer to their deepest needs; that He was the answer to the perennial problems of sin and evil, suffering and death; He was the acrostical *ITHOS* (Jesus Christ, Son of God, Savior).

The Church as the Gathered and Scattered People of God

The abiding monument to David Trumbull is the Union Church which he organized in 1846. This church, still bearing witness to the Gospel, is now located in Vina del Mar, an attractive suburb of Valparaiso, Chile. Across the years, even in the face of former persecution, Union Church has been the House of God for British, Scotch, North American, German, Spanish, and Chilean peoples who came and went from and to the four corners of the earth. The dual nature and role of the Church is well expressed in a report of the minister of Union Church to the sponsoring agency:

> At the close of thirty-two years it may be added that, while we have here assembled gathered from different portions of the earth, and differing nationally as well as denominationally, yet a remarkable measure of harmony has characterized our history. And if the past has not proved a failure, there is no reason to apprehend a less measure of success. Our fathers' principles have been crowned with good results during a score and a half years, and

they require nothing but energy and consistency on our part to
have them serve the same purpose for a century. We personally
may pass away, but others will rise up and take our places.(5)

Again the special role of the Union Church in Valparaiso,
Chile is recorded in the report of the apostle-founder to
the American and Foreign Gospel Union:

> Another peculiarity of this congregation has been the frequency
> of the changes taking place in it. There may not be ten persons
> connected with it today who belonged to it thirty years ago.
> Often, as soon as persons have come to be interested they have
> moved away. Although this has in it a measure of discouragement,
> still it has an advantage; the influence of the church is felt by
> a larger number than could be in a more stationary community. I
> judge that 2,500 persons have been connected with the congregation
> from the first day until now, 600 belonging to it at the present
> time; while the number of communicants during the same period
> will have ranged between 400 and 500, today 150 are upon the roll.
>
> From these facts the importance of our enterprise is evident to
> all. This society occupies a position that can be made one of
> widely extending influence. It stands at a point where there is
> an ebb and flow. People come and depart. It is for us to cast
> our bread upon the waters; we shall find it after many days.(6)

The ebb and flow nature and mission of the Church is re-
stated by David Trumbull in his counsel to the German
Lutheran Congregations in southern Chile:

> The purpose in founding the Chile Mission in 1845 was to draw to-
> gether the Foreign Protestant residents here, and to form a
> nucleus of evangelical life, of living atoms, of god-fearing
> believers, with whom and through whom the native circles were to
> be reached, souls converted, churches organized, preachers raised
> up and elders ordained until Chile should indeed become a part of
> the kingdom of our Lord Jesus Christ. What we have done in a
> measure in this city must be done in other points, in other sea-
> ports and in other towns. Really we trust the German contingent
> is now coming up to render holy and effective aid.(7)

These foreigners were for many years deprived of the
privilege of public worship and for this reason met in
their own homes or in the chapels of the foreign consulates.
The first Protestant service to be held in Valparaiso,
Chile, was in the home of a British merchant by the name
of John Sewall. He came to Chile from Madras, India, where
he had been engaged in business. He was a member of the
Episcopal Church. He had a chapel fitted up adjoining his
own dwelling.(8)

However meritorious was the private worship in the homes of the foreign dissidents, the Biblical mandate for public worship was bound to be obeyed. The title of the sermon preached by David Trumbull in Union Church, June 22, 1884 was "Mutual Influence in Public Worship." The text was "Consider one another to provoke unto love and to good works: not forsaking the assembling of yourselves together as the manner of some is"(Hebrews 10:24-25). By way of a biographical homily the minister set forth his model for the worshipping people of God.

> Among the earliest impressions of life are the recollections of public worship. Some of you can recall the faces of men you used to see in the church when you were children. They may not have been very learned but Sabbath after Sabbath they came to worship God; May not have been in all things consistent, but they were in their place when Sunday came. In my native town the Presbyterian congregation with which my parents attended, numbered about nine hundred: and I can at this distance recall, how staid farmers sat there who all the week had wrought hard and on the Sabbath morning harnessing their own teams had come two, three or four miles to wait upon the Lord. Cold weather did not keep them at home even when bleak winds swept over fields of snow. Nothing but a drenching storm or serious illness would show their seat vacant. I cannot say that they were always wakeful; a part of my amusement as a little chap was to watch some of them while they slept, to gaze at those who through infirmity or otherwise did it often. But it was a church-going community. For a family not to go to the Lord's house was an exception to the rule. It was rare for a man to be absent. Men did not say "this is Sunday, shall I go to church today, or stay home?", but they said "This is the Sabbath day and I am going." It was a thing habitual, a matter of course, and the effect was very perceptible; the power of association was felt, everybody was encouraged by everybody else to leave home and to wait on Jehovah statedly in the great congregation.(9)

Keep the Unity of the Spirit (Ephesians 4:3)

The minister of Union Church in Valparaiso, Chile, was a pioneer agent of the modern Ecumenical Movement. The Gospel Union, established in 1856, brought together the several Denominations working within the country. David Trumbull was the regional correspondent of the World's Evangelical Alliance which united fellow-Christians of a global community. In 1884, a call was sent for all to pray unitedly "to our adorable God and Father who cares for the nations, churches and individuals beset by tumults, uncertainities and anxieties."

The Gospel in the Reformed Tradition 93

Although this call went out so long ago it seems as though it is just as descriptive of and appropriate for our contemporary world. David Trumbull's professor at Princeton, Dr. Charles Hodge (1797-1878) wrote the *Basis of Faith* of the Evangelical Alliance in 1846.

The voluntary participation in the organization and program of activities of the Union Church of Valparaiso, Chile, makes it most appropriate to define the Church as "the People of God." The christian disciples of that community took seriously the Reformed doctrine of the "Christian Vocation" and the doctrine of "the Priesthood of Every Believer."

They were the ones who called and supported David Trumbull as minister of the Servant Church. They supported the Day Schools and the Sunday Schools with their money and personal ministries. They paid for the publication of *The Record* and for the thousands of religious tracts. They paid for the support of four colporteurs, for the Seamen's chaplaincy and for the Sheltering Home (orphanage). They were active members of the Missionary Society, The Temperance Society, the Y.M.C.A. and the Bible Society. One reads with amazement the way some of these christian laymen gave of their time and money to the cause of the Gospel. The biographer of the firm, Williamson Balfour and Associates portrays for us how some of these people dedicated themselves to the ministries of the church:

> After prayers we go to church at eleven o'clock, come out at the same time as at home and get up here to a two o'clock (cold) dinner which is often shared by a Captain or some stray body who has no home. We never invite any other kind of person. Mr. McCulloch does not come home to dinner as he has a Sunday School class to teach and a meeting for study of the Bible to attend in the evening.
>
> We remain reading in the afternoon and sometimes take a stroll by the watercourse or hillside. Mr. Williamson also devotes an hour to reading in Spanish from the Bible and explaining to the native servants along with any other Chilean he can persuade to come. Mr. Balfour spends a good part of the afternoon in reading to the sick in the English Hospital. Then after tea we go to church again at half past seven. And so our Sabbath ends. . .
>
> Many other deserving objects benefited from Stephen's and Alexander's time and money. They and their wives were frequent visitors at the hospitals. They helped with the soup kitchens after the bombardment. In 1881 they subscribed large sums for the care of those wounded or orphaned in the war of the Pacific. They maintained facilities for the sailors in the Port. They made loans to many charities. After review at the year's end,

these loans were often written off by payments from the Benevolent Fund.

Steven started a savings bank. He took an active interest in the Press, especially in the Record, a semi-religious publication in English which was gratuitously distributed, and delivered post free to the interior. . .

Alexander was one of the founders of the Y.M.C.A. in Chile. He was its honorary president from its inception until his death. He started a reading room for the English artisans, who gave him a most touching tea-party on his departure for home. He even sent out some larks, with minute instructions for their distribution, because Chile had so few singing birds. . . Steven and Alexander set an example in Chile which was a rare privilege for their successors to follow.(10)

The Gospel in Terms of Emancipation

The word "emancipation" runs like a theme song throughout the sermons and writings of David Trumbull. Just as the Chilean were so valiant and successful in winning their political independence from Spain, so also, he contended, they should with equal determination win their moral and spiritual independence from the Holy See. In this vein, he wrote:

> The question is whether the Chilean nation have or have not anything positive to say in the question of the revered presbyter who shall rule as archbishop over them. Let any European potentate assert a claim to interfere in the selection of their Chief Magistrate in political matters, and the manly out-spoken resistance, with which is claims will be met, will be in keeping with the lofty spirit of independence that has long ago characterized the Chilean people. They would resist to the uttermost; every man and every woman would rise up in arms to maintain the refusal to submit to such domination.

> How is it then in regards to a Chief Prelate in church matters? In this, one might feel that he had come into another nation. The people who were so self-asserting and so brave, are now found willing to go cap in hand, knocking at the door of a ruler who dwells in Italy, soliciting his consent that they may have over them in the Lord the man of their choice. Independent enough in other things here they have asked, waited, supplicated, sought interviews, prayed, besought and cringed, till on-lookers have felt moved to pity them.(11)

The above quotation raised the issue of the prolonged and basic conflict between the Church and the State. The Church did not concede that the sovereign State of Chile had the right of National Patronage. When Archbishop Rafael Valdivieso died in July of 1878, the Chilean Council of State chose the liberal priest Paula Tafaró to take his place. The Pope rejected this nomination and sent Monsenor Celestino del Frate to settle the conflict. In spite of every effort to settle the affair neither the Church nor the Government would accept the claims of the other. President Domingo Santa Maria (1881-1886) then gave the Apostolic Delegate his passports on January 15, 1883. The Archbishopric of Santiago remained vacant until 1887 when Mariano Casanova was preconized by the Vatican under the administration of President Jose Manuel Balmacea (1886-1891). This was one of four occasions when the Chilean government exiled Papal delegates because of their refusal to recognize National Patronage.(12)

"Emancipation," according to David Trumbull, more than political independence, was also applicable to freedom of thought and freedom of expression. In his day not many dared to challenge the tyranny of the ultramontanes who arrogated to themselves the exclusive tutelage of both the spiritual and secular affairs of the nation. For them the man from Connecticut was a thorn in the flesh. He dared to challenge the authority of "the only true Church" and to provoke a public debate of the issues which gave rise to the Protestant Reformation. The liberal daily papers such as *El Mercurio*, *El Ferrocarril*, and *La Voz de Chile* published and informed the general public of the controversy, usually favoring religious tolerance and reform. *La Revista Catolica* was established in 1843 to offset the defense of the dissidents. The arguments of the dominant Church were; that a non-Catholic religion would be detrimental to national unity; that it would offend the traditional sentiments of the masses and that it would give rise to indifference, agnosticism, and immorality. In the discipline of polemics, David Trumbull was well prepared. His political involvement was always restrained by his piety, humility, and candor. His gentility was somewhat disarming to his most ardent adversary.

One of the effective means of the dissemination of the Reformed ideology was the wide use of religious tracts. To this end the American Tract Society came to his aid. Founded in 1825, its stated purpose as recorded in Article I of its Constitution was as follows:

> This Society shall be denominated the *American Tract Society*; the object of which shall be to diffuse a knowledge of our Lord Jesus Christ as the redeemer of sinners, and to promote the interests of vital goodness and sound morality, by the circulation of Religious Tracts, calculated to receive the approbation of all Evangelical Christians.(13)

Of the hundred of thousands of Tracts published by the said Society and scattered widely in Chile is one written by David Trumbull entitled "Who Will Give Rain." The story is brifely retold by Florence E. Smith, missionary in Chile from 1894 to 1958, as follows:

> In 1863 there was a prolonged drought in Chile such as was repeated in 1924. Harvests failed and animals died by the thousands. The patron saint of rain, St. Isidor, was appealed to in public petition, processions, and so forth, and suddenly an abundant rain fell. Some thanked the Virgin, some saint Isidor, some saint Bartholomew, but the editor of the *Voz de Chile* suggested that perhaps atmospheric conditions had something to do with saving the country. Mariano Casanova, ecclesiastical governor of Valparaiso and afterwards archbishop of Chile, wrote an article in *El Ferrocarril* defending the worship of saints and attributing to them power to confer celestial benefits on believers.
>
> Once more David Trumbull entered the lists, answering Casanova in an article published in *La Voz de Chile*, "Who Sends Rain?" terminating with the citation of Zechariah 10:1-2 "Ask ye of the Lord rain in the time of the latter rain; so the Lord shall make bright clouds, and give them showers of rain, to every one grass in the field. For the idols have spoken vanity, and the diviners have seen a lie, and have told false dreams; they comfort in vain; therefore they went their way as a flock, they were troubled, because there was no shepherd."
>
> A few days later he resumed the theme under three heads: Should we claim the intercession of the saints with God? Should we render them worship? Should we pray to their images?(14)

Such an apparent disparagement of the precepts and practices of the Church was bound to provoke wide discussion and in the end liberate many souls from the aberrations of obscurantism. Traditions and religious sentiments which were subject to reform and liberation are realistically described by historian, Ricardo Donoso in a chapter on "The Struggle Against the Influence of the Church."

> Of the total spiritual legacy Spain gave to the Hispanic-American Society none was more important than the influence of the Catholic Church. The activities of the religious orders and of the Inquisition not only contributed to the formation of a strong religious sentiment but also gave rise to a narrow fanaticism whose open manifestations were reflected holidays, religious festivals, processions and petitions. Natural cataclysms, the overflowing of rivers, torrential down-pours, earthtremors and earthquakes gave rise to noisy and exalted manifestations of religious feeling, during which there were excessive outcries, tears and general groanings. The common people had a blind faith in the miracles which were attributed to all the saints of the calendar but also

whom they venerated with simple and fervent faith in the miraculous power of their images, such as the Virgin of Succor, which was kept in the San Francisco Church, the Lord of May of the Agustinians, the Virgin of Andacollo and many other saints which were venerated throughout the entire Republic. . . In this respect, Chile, in her development and struggle for emancipation was no different than other Hispanic-American countries, much to the surprise of travelers who had occasion to visit them. No struggle then, was so disruptive than that which was to tear down the building which was so patiently erected by the endeavors of the authorities of the church, and to succeed to obtain not only freedom of expression but also religious tolerance. The story of these efforts constitutes one of the most passionate episodes of the political history of Chile.(15)

The Gospel in Terms of Social Concern and Action

In his sermon on "A Servant of Jesus Christ," Romans 1:1, David Trumbull said, "To serve Christ is to reform society, is to console the sorrowful, to instruct the ignorant and lead to repentance such as are estranged from God." This understanding of the Biblical injunction was never so clearly expressed as in the concern for addicts of alcoholism and the dire social consequences. The Rev. Lyman Beecher and Rev. Leonard Bacon, supporters of the Temperance Movement and moral monitors of David Trumbull when a student at Yale College, persuaded their disciple that total abstention was the best cure for pernicious effects of rum and other ardent liquors.(16) There was no reason to wonder then why David Trumbull made Temperance an essential part of his "errand in the wilderness." As chaplain of the American Seamen's Friend Society he was often confronted with inebriety as a besetting sin of seamen who had not found any other alternative to the rigors and privations of prolonged sea-voyages. But temperance was not only for sailors. Children were enrolled in "The Band of Hope" and for older folk the Local Lodges were chapters of a worldwide Temperance Movement. Templar Lodge Number I of Chile was an integral part of the program of activities of Union Church, Valparaiso. At one of the frequent meetings of the Lodge, David Trumbull said:

> The Good Templars are engaged in a work, in the success of which all men ought to be interested. . . If men and women could be induced to their duty, in regard to temperance, thousands might be redeemed from drunkenness, many families might be made happy by the restoration of husbands and fathers to soberness and duty, many hearts be made light that are burdened with woe at the impending ruin of dear friends and relatives. The principles of the Good Templar Order are: total abstinence by life-long pledges, and the absolute prohibition of the manufacturing, importation, and sale of intoxicating drinks.(17)

In view of David Trumbull's stance on Temperance and strict observance of keeping the Sabbath, no doubt there were those who thought of him as a dour Puritan of the Victorian Age. Yet others found that his austerity did not negate his genial and jovial character. One who knew him well paid the following tribute to the minister of Union Church, Valparaiso:

> The early period at which Doctor Trumbull came to Chile, the difficulties he had to encounter, his fearlessness, tenacity, wisdom, tack, and many other qualities of excellence, his success where failure must often have been predicted, make of this man a strickingly prominent figure. It is impossible to estimate the meed of praise due to him for educating the legislators of Chile in matters pertaining to religious liberty; his relations with all were more than kindly, evincing affection for every fellow-creature and charity for faults and errors; he strove to reclaim by entreaty, instead of denunciation; his domestic and daily life made him attractive to those with whom he came in contact; for those in trials there were ever-ready words of cheer and hope. Having a keen appreciation for humor, his countenance was as frequently irradiated with smiles as were the tones of his voice brightened by merry, quiet laughter; a volume would hardly suffice for the anedotes told by or of him. Of his powers of repartee I will cite one, possibly little known:
>
> Travelling on one occasion between New York and Valparaiso, the steamer grounded -- I believe on one of the Florida reefs; it became evident that the ship, passengers and crew would probably be lost if the situation was not soon favorably altered; feelings of gloom mastered all on board. A couple of the passengers, who had known the Doctor to induce others to become the same, had ordered a bottle of cognac, and, as the dominie slowly passed back and forth in front of them in the dining saloon, his mind given up to the reflection natural in moments so serious, were occupying themselves in making and taking draughts of "Dutch courage." Thinking the moment opportune to employ a little "chaft" on the Doctor, both assumed airs of nonchalance as to what might soon occur; each time he passed where they were seated he was saluted with expressions like, "Doctor, have a nip! Nothing like a good horn of cognac, Doctor at a time like this! Do give it a trial, Doctor!" In vain the Dominie replied to these invitations in expressions like "Thank you, gentlemen, I beg you will excuse me. I can get along very well without it;" the molestation continued. At last, stopping in front and facing them, at an additional request -- or jibe -- he quietly replied, "I am very much obliged gentlemen, but *I am not frightened enough yet!*" The invitations most suddenly ceased. (18)

The concern of David Trumbull for the cause of Temperance turned out to be of utmost importance to Chile and for international relations. The unfortunate "Baltimore

Affaire" deftly describes the dire consequences of a drunken brawl on the streets of Valparaiso in 1891:

> One unhappy legacy from the Civil War was the ugly dispute with the United States over the "Baltimore Affair." The American cruiser U.S.S. Baltimore had put into Valparaiso harbor and her captain unwisely permitted his sailors to disembark. The United States, openly favorable to Balmaceda, was already in bad odor with the Chilean people. The visiting sailors, tongues loosed by rum, soon were involved in a street fight. Two Americans were killed, several were wounded, while the police looked on. The result was an ultimatum from Secretary of State James G. Blaine demanding apologies, the firing of guns in salute to the American flag, and idemnity for the victims. Montt refused to comply, and the Chilean population demanded war with the United States. However, being a realistic man, he then ordered $75,000 paid to the families of the dead, and the incident was officially closed; but Chile long remembered it as an affront to the national dignity.(19)

Even in contemporary Chile, alcoholism is a serious health problem for the nation. A friendly critic reports the situation as follows:

> Chilean doctors and students of social conditions have long been convinced that the per-capita alcohol consumption is higher in Chile than in any other Latin American country. The striking fact of this situation is that the upper and middle classes are, it is commonly agreed, reasonably temperate. This means that the lower classes must do much more than their share in driving up consumption figures. This seems in particular to be a function of the lower-class men -- for their women are not noted for drinking in excesses. In various urban slum areas it is estimated that from 20 per cent to 30 per cent of the men are chronic drunkards, who can be expected to spend the majority of weekends on prolonged binges.(20)

Given the gravity of this situation, today, there are thousands of heirs of the Reformed Tradition who are persuaded that the *Band of Hope* and the principles and practices of the Good Templar Lodge Esmeralda No. I of Chile are the answer to the personal and social problems of alcoholism.

From this brief summary of the Gospel in the Reformed Tradition, it may be said that, for its agent, piety and politics were inextricably joined and that, in some measure, his life and works influenced the matrix and web of the personal socioeconomic and cultural life of the developing nation-state.

9
ADVOCATE OF CONSTITUTIONAL REFORMS

Article V of the original project of the Chilean Constitution stated that, "the Roman Apostolic and Catholic Religion is and always will be the religion of the State." Joel Roberts Poinsett, United States representative in Chile and counselor to the Supreme leader of the emerging Republic, General José Miguel Carrera, advised in 1811 that the word "Roman" be omitted. The mere suggestion of such a change provoked a heated and prolonged debate and gave rise to the historical political parties, conservatives and liberals of the nation.(1) Heman Allen, diplomatic agent of the United States in 1824, endeavored to persuade the Chilean legislators to omit Article V of the several previous Constitutions. He advocated religious tolerance and argued that a State Religion was not appropriate to a Republic. The dominance and hostility of the clergy "was so great that not one of the deputies to Congress dared to vote for the revision for fear of being assassinated."(2)

The refusal of the Church to recognize the right of National Patronage and the pre-emption of religious tolerance as stipulated by Article V of the 1833 Constitution set the state for a long and bitter conflict between the Church and the State. The religious issue continued to be the apple of discord throughout the history of the developing nation. A Chilean historian writes:

> In 1878 Rafael Valentín Valdivieso, head of the Chilean Church for thirty years, died in Santiago. No priest ever left the country better memories for virtue and charity. His whole life had been a constant struggle not only in behalf of his faith but, more than

that, in behalf of the poor to whom he gave what he had, even sacrificing for them every comfort and pleasure. But this humble and kindly man became harsh and unyielding when he thought the prerogatives of his Church were attacked. More than once therefore, he saw himself enveloped in bitter conflicts with civil authority, whose right of 'ecclesiastical patronage' he accepted only under protest on every occasion when it was exercised. For this reason the Government at his death desired to fill his place with a priest who would be a pledge of harmony between Church and State. It actually elected Canon Francisco de Paula Taforo, also an eminent churchman of blameless life but possessed of outstanding liberal ideas, and proposed him to the pope for appointment. The clergy of Santiago and the conservative party were alarmed; they opposed the selection and succeeded in having the pope withhold the nomination.(3)

Given the constitutional privileges and protection of the State-Church, the latter practically was in charge of the civil register of the vital statistics, the use of the cemeteries, the arbiter of mixed marriages, the control of religious instruction in the public schools and the right of the clergy to be tried in ecclesiastical courts. The many dissenters in Chile were greatly annoyed and often humiliated by these statutes and, in that they were considered to be unreasonable and contrary to inalienable human rights, they were, at times willfully disobeyed.

In 1877 David Trumbull wrote a four part defense of "Mixed Marriages" which was published in the daily newspaper *La Voz de Chile* (The Voice of Chile). This was in answer to a young editor of *La Revista Católica* (The Catholic Review). This man at the age of eighty became the Archbishop of Santiago and in 1925 negotiated for the new Constitution and the peaceful separation of Church and State.

Advocating constitutional changes of the marriage laws of Chile in 1877 David Trumbull wrote:

> As long ago as 1849 we pleaded through the press that this demoralizing state of affairs might be taken in hand by Congress and changed in favor of equity and toleration; and it was then promised changes should be introduced so as to permit mixed marriages without sacrificing the dignity of either man or woman, and without consigning innocent children any longer to the shame of illegitimacy. But today, in 1877, after more than a quarter of a century, the same falsehoods have to be uttered, the same lies told, the same hypocritical professions made, the same enforced and sacrilegious baptisms gone through with or else dispensations brought, or else immoral relations formed -- if persons who are not Romanists would be married with those who are.(4)

A case in point which reflected this distressing discrimination of foreign and national dissidents was one which disrupted diplomatic relations between Chile and the United States for an entire year. In the 1840's Seth Barton, United States Minister to chile, became involved in a dispute with the Archbishop of Santiago, Rafael Valentín Valdivieso. He wanted to marry a Chilean lady of a distinguished aristocratic family and promised to bring up their children as Catholics. The prelate doubted his sincerity and tried to persuade the prospective bride that such a marriage would be sacrilegious. He insisted that she should repent and return to the Roman Catholic faith. Recriminating letters were written by Prelate and Minister. In the end the couple were married by a chaplain of the United States Navy but not before Henry Clay, the United States Secretary of State, recalled his Minister.(5)

The Secularization of the Cemeteries

From the earliest days of the establishment of the Chilean Republic, the quarrel between the Church and the State over the matter of the secularization of the cemeteries gave rise to an acrimonious controversy which lasted for fifty years.(6) One of the complaints the power elite made against the Supreme Director, Bernardo O'Higgins was that he made it possible for the Protestants of Valparaiso to provide for their own cemetery. He was greatly embarrassed in confessing this intolerance to Maria Graham, wife of a British Naval Officer and a friend of the Supreme Director. The following conversation is taken from her interview in 1822:

> He conversed freely about the state of Chile, and told me he doubted not that I must be surprised at the backwardness of the country in many things, and particularly mentioned the want of religious toleration, or, the very measure of it which, considering the general state of things, he had yet been able to grant, without disturbing the public tranquility; and he seemed a little inclined to censure those Protestants who wished prematurely to force upon him the building a chapel, and the public institution of Protestant worship; forgetting how very short a time it is since even private liberty of conscience and a consecrated burial-place had been allowed in a country which, within twelve years, had been subjected to the Inquisition in Lima. He spoke a good deal also of the necessity of public education, and told me of the Lancasterian and other schools lately established here, and other towns in Chile, which are certainly numerous in proportion to the population.((7)

In that the "blessed" cemeteries were restricted to the burial of those who were in good standing with the Roman

Catholic Church and permission controlled by the local priest, the Protestants were obliged to bury their dead without funeral rites outside the walls of the cemeteries, on the beaches or in some wasteland. This deplorable situation was the concern of a letter of the United States Minister, Heman Allen, of August 24, 1824, to the Chilean Minister of Foreign Relations, which in part was as follows:

> The Plenipotential Minister of the United States has the honor of reporting to the Minister of Foreign Relations that he sadly observes that, because of the laws and customs of Chile, his fellow citizens and other foreigners are deprived of the free exercise of their usual funeral and burial services; that he has known that in some instances some shameful indecencies have been committed with the bodies of their fellow citizens, and for this reason he himself is obliged, in fulfillment of his duty in representing the citizens of the United States, to respectfully call attention to the government of Chile concerning the need to provide some law for the protection of those privileges to which they are accustomed. It should be understood that this has to do with those who actually reside in Chile and those who may be in transit.(8)

The foreign colony in Santiago, Chile obtained permission only by way of a treaty agreement to establish their own cemetery. For thirty years they were obliged to transfer their dead to the dissident cemetery in the port city of Valparaiso. If unable to bear the expense of such a transfer the dissidents were forced to bury their dead on the rock hill of Santa Lucia where criminals and paupers were interred. In later years the liberal mayor of the city, don Vicuna Mackenna, transfered the bodies to a public cemetery and erected a simple monument to "the memory of those exiles from heaven and earth who in this place lay buried for half a century, 1820-1870."(9)

During the administration of President Domingo Santa Maria (1881-1886) a project for the secularization of the cemeteries, which he himself had advocated in 1872, was made a constitutional statute. After a long and passionate debate in the Congress the law was passed on August 2, 1883. The State-Church was no longer in control of the cemeteries and provision was made for their free use by all religious communities.(10)

This period of Chilean history is known as that of the "Theological Reforms."(11) Several radical changes of the Constitution were made for the purpose of diminishing the dominance of the Church in matters pertaining to the secular society.(12) In 1875 the clergy were deprived of the privilege of being tried for civil delinquencies in ecclesiastical courts. On January 16, 1884 the law of Civil

Marriage was approved by the Congress. This meant that the Church lost the traditional authority to legally establish the family.

On January 16, 1884, the law of Civil Registration was made a part of the Constitution. This law rescinded the authority of the Church to register the birth, marriage, and death of all the inhabitants of the nation. "So great was the opposition made everywhere by the clergy against these laws," writes historian Luis Galdames, ". . .that the country seemed on the verge of a revolution."(13) These Reforms were stigmatized by the hierchy as "sacriligious" and those who voted for them were threatened with excommunication."(14) On the other hand, senator Vicuna MacKenna said "it was a declaration of the second Independence of the Nation."(15)

President Santa Maria, in his annual address to the Congress on June 1, 1884, expressed his satisfaction with the ardous labors and the passage of the Reform Laws as follows:

> Necessary it is that you, Fellow-citizens of the Senate and the House of Deputies, terminate with the skill and the prudent courage which you have manifested, the work commenced in your sittings of last year, so that the laws touching Marriage and Civil Registration may be carried into execution without hindrance. I congratulate myself on the important victories the nation has achieved in this direction. The laws to which I refer to do not intend to diminish nor to bar any right, less still to wound any religious belief, since all among us enjoy the most complete legal protection. It was not possible to continue longer under the abnormal regime which, frustrating the rights of many, constantly produced annoying controversies that disturbed the peace of families and violated the consciences of individuals. Today the law rules alike for all, though leaving a broad and sure field to religious belief.
>
> The completion of the Law of Civil Registration will make it easy to carry into effect that of Civil Marriage; and in this way, without injuring or deriding religious marriage for those who desire it, the forming of the family will no longer encounter irritating obstacles. . .These practical results should not be imperiled by an immediate effort for more "extreme measures," i.e. the separation of Church and State.(16)

The reaction of David Trumbull to these Constitutional Reforms was unique in the history of intercultural relations. He had given the best of his life in advocating such changes and he had made a vow that if these laws were passed in the Congress he would become a Chilean citizen. To serve as a catalytic agency in uniting the Anglo and Latin American cultures was an act of supreme devotion. Dr. Robert E.

Speer, Secretary of the Presbyterian Board of Foreign Missions gave the following account of this historic event:

> So deeply had his interest been enlisted in the contest and so intensely had he entered into the life of the land that he had vowed that if the cemetery and marriage reforms passed he would become a Chilean citizen. When this desire of his heart was fulfilled, he "appeared," as one of the Valparaiso newspapers says, "before the municipality, asking for naturalization papers; on hearing this petition, one of the municipal officers, in manifestation of the wishes of all, requested that a note be entered in the record of the pleasure with which as a body they received Dr. Trumbull's application, and asked that, without the legal formality of placing it on the table, it should be at once forwarded to the President of the Republic. This was unanimously sustained." He had long been accustomed to refer to Chile as "our country" and to its institutions and interest as his own, and his naturalization naturally strengthened the feelings of affection and confidence with which Chileans regarded him. The great-grandson of Jonathan Trumbull was a loyal American to the last drop of his blood. That was why, being in Chile, knowing that Chile was to be his home, he sought to live wholly for Chile, and to bring into the very blood of Chile his own life by what he looked upon as the sacrament of naturalization.(17)

The liberal forces in the national Congress readily accepted David Trumbull as a Chilean citizen. He in fact was their frequent consultant in the principles of government relating to the Reform Laws. It is believed that his understudy, the Rev. José Manuel Ibañez Guzmán, wrote the draft for the Law of Civil Registration.(18) Soon after the promulgation of the Marriage law the citizens of Valparaiso honored President Santa Maria with a banquet. At that time the Secretary of State, Jose Manuel Balmaceda, said:

> A breath of higher inspiration moved the constituted powers of the State, and the walls of Jerico have fallen, the regimen of privilege, official fanaticism and religious oppression, in the name of faith, have come to an end. The reign of conscience and religious equality has now begun.(19)

José Manuel Balmaceda succeeded Domingo Santa Maria and was president of Chile from 1886 to 1889. After the prolonged controversy with the Church concerning the appointment of the new Archbishop, the "Theological Questions," the war with Peru and Bolivia (1879-1884), the new president sought to unite the political factions and to promote the peace and prosperity of the nation. Toward this end he expedited the appointment of Mariano Casanova, the ecclesiastical governor of Valparaiso, as successor to Archbishop Rafael Valdivieso in the leadership of the Church. Casanova was the prelate who carried on the public discussion with

David Trumbull as to the role of the saints in sending rain and also the one who was opposed to the distribution of the Vaughan New Testaments.

Striving for the ideal of a Free Church within a Free State, Balmaceda had organized a "Reform Club." In response to the idea of separation of Church and State and the exclusive Article V of the Constitution, Casanoa in his pastoral letter of April 1, 1888 wrote "such an act would be a terrible calamity; it would divide the Chilean family; it would be contrary to morality; it would be contrary to the teaching of religion and would raise up a monster State without God."(20)

Given the intransigeance of the head of the Church, the president's ideal had to wait for years to come. Under the circumstances, David Trumbull was not in favor of relinquishment of the National Patronage. His colleague, W. E. Dodge explained the unfortunate failure of the legislation to separate Church and State. In a letter to the Presbyterian Board of Mission on May 11, 1888 he wrote, "The reform of the fifth or religious article of the Constitution had been voted by two congresses and we hoped it would be finally passed by the third and become the law of the land. At the last moment however, party differences arose on other grounds, and this, together with renewed priestly opposition, has defeated the measure so long looked for by the friends of religious freedom. . . Ultimately we hope the reform will be passed. At present, under the liberal government we have faint hope to secure a charter to hold property but we do not feel confident of success. (21)

The "faint hope" however was not warranted, for soon, the Mission Board was informed of the legal incorporation of *La Unión Evangélica* (Evangelical Union) by a decree dated November 5, 1888. The letter stated, "This was Dr. Trumbull's last work in connection with the Mission, and it was the crown; for it placed all evangelical work on a legal basis, and practically granted not merely the Presbyterian Mission, but all other organizations laboring in Chile, freedom of worship.(22)

The Reformed Church was illegal in Chile from the time of its establishment in 1847. Not until Article V of the 1833 Constitution was, by popular consent, changed to Article X of the 1925 new Constitution was there complete freedom and equality for all religious communities. In no small measure the peaceful separation of Church and State was due to the foundation laid by David Trumbull. Article X of the present Constitution reads, "The Constitution insures to all the inhabitants of the Republic the practice of all beliefs, liberty of conscience and the free exercise of all religions that may not be contrary to morality, good use and public order. Therefore, the respective religious bodies have the right to erect and maintain houses of worship and accessory property under the conditions of security and hygiene as fixed by the laws and regulations.(23)

All these Constitutional Reforms, after all, were an end product of the 16th Century Reformation Movement and in keeping with the spirit of the 1st Century Liberator who said "And ye shall know the truth, and the truth shall make you free" (John 8:32, K.J.V.).

10

MISSION ACCOMPLISHED

"Wherefore, let them that suffer according to the will of God, commit the keeping of their souls unto him in well doing, as unto a faithful Creator" (I Peter 4:19, KJV)

This biblical text was the subject of a sermon preached by David Trumbull early in his ministry in Chile but published in *The Record* only after he entered "the rest which remaineth for the people of God." In retrospect, it would appear to have been autobiographical. He was persuaded that God had called him to well doing by way of creative suffering. This understanding of his mission is noted in the words of his sermon: . . .to the good man God is a new Creator: as it were his second Creator, who has created him unto good works, unto well doing. It is through the influence of his Creator on his mind that he lives according to his will. . . He who has renewed his soul will give to him a great reward and perfect safety. . . All who live unto God must suffer . . .no person will become a child of God without suffering something.(1)

Letters and tributes record for all time the trials and triumpths of this man of God. His self-image of sacrificial sacrifice is evident in the 1842 Class Letter of Yale College. In response to an invitation to attend the Class Reunion of 1887, David Trumbull wrote:

Here comes your postal invitation. O, if I could but have been there! But don't go as a missionary to foreign parts if you desire to keep close and frequent intercourse with classmates, or even relatives. I trust that the occasion was felicitous, and that many enjoyed it, even though I could not; and shall look forward with interest to your published account of the meeting, and shall devour every word of it with avidity. 'Do they miss me at home?' is the phrase that comes to my exiled mind.

Today I have felt wearied, having been out collecting for local Bible Society, and worried because of troubles of others, who had appealed to me for justice in matters out of my control; and your postal has come in to at least alleviate and make me feel more complacent regarding this rough and cold world.

I am having my sermons translated into Spanish -- eighteen of them having been already printed -- and four in manuscript wait their turn.

I have been pastor of this flock, the Union Church, for forty-two years come next Christmas. If any one can outbid that let me know his name and abode, and give my love to him. To you I send it anyhow, for the pains you have taken to keep bright the links of the chain that ought to bind us together in our age, when we near the end of the race, as it did when we were boys at the beginning of it.

I should like to be spared to the Lord thirteen years longer, always provided I keep my wits; then on the coming in of the new century, I should say 'Now lettest thou thy servant depart in peace.' I doubt if I shall ever again see my native country, as much as I love it and thank it for all it has done for me; although if, in 1892, I might meet those that remain, it would be a joy and a consolation.(2)

The "errand in the wilderness" was accomplished sooner than David Trumbull had wished, for on the very day he entered into "Immanuel's Land" he sent the following message to the classmates of his Alma Mater, "I am in my bed, unable to write, and ask my daughter to do it, merely to say to my dear classmates and secretary, that during the last month I have experienced renewed and severe attacks of the heart, which first came in 1879, and from which I have since had a measure of relief which has let me do part of my work. It is not so now. I am very weak -- can't rise from my bed without distress in breathing, and exertion brings angina on. I do not think my Heavenly Landlord intends making any more repairs on my tenement. I beg of you to convey to the class my fraternal regards and assure them that if our lives have been widely separated, I have always wished them the very best of things, and heard of their welfare with pleasure. Should God disappoint my fears, and spare me still, I shall let you know." (3)

Tributes ascribed to David Trumbull speak eloquently of a Mission Accomplished. Dr. Robert E. Speer, Secretary of the Board of Foreign Missions of the Presbyterian Church and who chose him as one of six missionary statesmen wrote, "the pioneer missionary. . .deserves to be every remembered for his service in securing a liberalization of the laws of Chile, in promoting a wide range of thought and sympathy, in uplifting the tone of a foreign community in a comercial city, and embodying high ideals of noble and companionable character. In all South America we found no foreign community so happily interrelated or so well maintaining home ideals and religious institutions as the foreign community in Valparaiso."(4)

At the memorial service held at Union Church in Valparaiso, February 10, 1889, a colleague said, "In the service of his Divine Master he looked out upon Chile, nay upon this entire coast, as a field in which, so far as his influence and effort could reach, he should make known the glorious Gospel of Jesus Christ. To this end he labored not only in the grand work of his church and pulpit, but also in connection with various gospelizing agencies, as the Valparaiso Bible Society, The Seamen's Mission and the Chile Mission, representing the American Presbyterian Church in the land, and every other way possible."(5)

The secular daily newspaper *El Mercurio* wrote, "Valparaiso owed him much and she has always felt honored in calling him, first, as the most worthy and best of her foreign residents, and secondly, as a fellow countryman: nay, even more as a true brother as he proved by his love and interest which he felt in all that pertained to the material and moral advancement of this our country."(6)

The *Heraldo* of Valparaiso wrote, "He came to awaken our new life as a free people, and to strive against the prejudices of a society which was unwilling to recognize the excellence of any other than one single form of worship, and was to grant privileges solely to the ministers of the State religion. . . It was an entire revolution that he wrought in our country; he himself was an utter revolutionist; and yet before his life closed, he could not walk our streets without being saluted on all sides with tokens of respect, beloved and esteemed by all as a good man, in the full meaning of that phrase."(7)

Finally, in memory of this Yankee Reformer, foreigners and Chileans engraved on a marble shaft which marks his grave, the inscription:

Memoria Sacrum, The Reverend David Trumbull, D.D., Founder and Minister of the Union Church of Valparaiso. Born in Elizabeth, New Jersey, the 1st of November 1819. Died in Valparaiso the 1st of February, 1889. For forty-three years he gave himself to unwearied and successful effort in the cause of evangelical truth and religious liberty in this country. As a gifted and faithful minister, and as a friend he was honored and loved by foreign residents on this coast. In his public life he was the counselor of statesmen, the supporter of every good enterprise, the helper of the poor and the consoler of the afflicted.

In memory of his eminent services, charity and sympathy this monument has been raised by his friends in this community and by the citizens of his adopted country.(8)

11

EPILOGUE

Blessed are the dead which die in the Lord from henceforth: Yea, saith the Spirit that they may rest from their labors; and their works do follow them (Revelation 11:13, KJV)

The periodical called *The Record* was published for eighteen years under the direction of David Trumbull. After his name was inscribed in the Book of Life, *The Record* continued to publish some of his sermons. The sermon text for July 23, 1875, was as recorded above, which suggests an appropriate epilogue to the Life and Work of David Trumbull. The subheading of the issue for August 10, 1889, was "He being dead yet speaketh."

  Little did the author of the sermon envision the dramatic changes which were taking place in Chile even before the *Aggiornamento Movement* was initiated at the Second Vatican Council, 1963-65. When Pius XII issued his encyclical *Divino Afflante Spiritu* in 1943, prominent lay Catholics in Chile were directing serious studies of the once forbidden Book. Today there is hardly a news-stand in Santiago or Valparaiso where one cannot purchase, at a modicum price, beautiful pictorial copies of the Holy Scriptures. When the Catholic hierarchy give their *Nihil Obstat* and *Imprimatur* to common versions of the Bible, as they now do, it is in order to say that we are witnessing the end of the Catholic Counter Reformation.(1)

  A second dramatic change in the Protestant-Catholic confrontation is the invitation for dialogue and cooperation

Epilogue

initiated in Chile by the Bishop of Talca, Manuel Larrain Errazuriz. In the 1940's he invited the American-founded Order of the Maryknoll to establish in his country the comprehensive parish program. This ministry since then has re-vitalized the entire Church. The Bishop started a program of agrarian reform which has now been accepted as a major concern of the national government. He became a symbol of ecumenical Christianity in Latin America. He was one of the founders in 1963 of the Catholic Inter-American Cooperation Program, known as CICOP. This enterprise has become a joint crusade of North and South America Catholics on behalf of an integral program of evangelization.

David Trumbull would have been pleased to hear the explanation of the role of CICOP from the Prelate of Talca, Chile, especially in view of the persecution of a pioneer Yankee Reformer in that same city. The interpretation of the beloved and now the late* Bishop Larrain was as follows:

> This dialogue, promoted by CICOP, is one of the clearest indications that the people of North and South America, as well as the Catholics of their respective Churches, rising above the divisions which separate them, must learn to accomplish together the common destiny to which Providence call them.
>
> This dialogue to which CICOP calls us requires a resolution of the misunderstandings which have separated us for so long a time. This mutual misunderstanding is a painful fact.
>
> The common image of the Latin American and of Latin American Catholicism has no basis in reality. The same can be said of the inadequate appreciation of the spiritual values of North Americans which is widespread on the southern continent.
>
> Because CICOP calls us to this dialogue, because we know that God speaks to us through history, because we feel that this encounter between peoples and civilizations in search of unity is one of the great indications of the divine presence in the world -- for all these reasons -- we feel that CICOP is a 'sign of the times'. Even more precisely it is an echo of the Divine voice calling us to mutual understanding and union.(2)

In view of the many years of religious intolerance and opposition to the establishment of the Reformed Church in Chile it would appear as nothing less than a miracle of God that in these days a recognition of the Protestant ethic and the call for Catholic-Protestant cooperation should be made by distinguished Catholic historians and sociologists,

---

* The Bishop was killed when his automobile crashed into a horsedrawn cart at Rosario, Chile June 22, 1966.

Frederick B. Pike, Associate Professor of History at the University of Notre Dame and co-author of a recent volume on *Religion, Revolution and Reform: New Forces for Change in Latin America*, makes the following evaluation of the sociological research of Father Roger E. Vekemans:

> The Belgian Jesuit with many years of experience in Chile. . . has in effect said that unless the Catholic Church can undergo a cultural mutation that will cause it to stress the capitalistic virtues commonly associated with the Protestant ethic, then there may be no possibility of a non-Marxist solution for the problems of Latin America. He feels that in many parts of Europe because of its contact with Protestantism from the time of the Reformation, the Catholic Church at an early period went through this cultural mutation, and he desires to see the process repeated in today's Latin America.
>
> In many ways I am hopeful that the sort of cultural mutation of which Father Vekemans speaks with the Catholic Church coming to accept and disseminate the natural virtues stressed primarily in the past within the context of the Protestant Ethic, will be facilitated by an expanding role of Protestantism in Latin America.
>
> At the time of the Reformation, a titanic struggle was waged between two forces, Protestantism and Catholicism, both of which were spiritual and Christian. As a result, the influence of Christianity, either in one form or another, was not immediately threatened with extinction. One of the most titanic struggles underway in today's Latin America pits a force of atheistic materialism against one that defends spiritual, theistic values. I do not see how the tide of atheistic materialism can be successfully contained and rolled back unless Catholicism, as well as its increasingly important potential partner in Christianity, Protestantism, and its potential partner in spiritual and theistic values, Judaism, become more and more actual partners.(3)

There is a consensus among modern Latin American historians and social scientists which holds that when it is a matter of tolerance, of representative government and stability and progress, Chile is quite advanced in comparison with other Latin American Republics. Not many academicians however recognize that the contemporary cultural mutation is the end-product of the gestation period which began at the dawn of the 19th century when the native and foreign forerunners of the Reformed Church confronted a different cultural tradition and pattern. One distinguished person who did appreciate the influence of the Protestant culture and tradition on those of Chile was the present Cardinal Raul Silva Henriquez. In a conversation with John A. MacKay, former president of the Presbyterian Board of Missions, the Cardinal expressed his appreciation "for

Epilogue

what Protestant Missions and Protestant churches had contributed to the spiritual life of Latin America, and his gratitude for the debt which the Roman Catholic Church owed to them because of their vision and creative work." (4)

Another candid recognition of the moral and spiritual influence of the Protestant Church in Chile was the appraisal made by Father Ignacio Vergara in his meritorious study entitled "Protestantism in Chile." In 1963 he wrote:

> The purpose of this study is to make known Protestantism in Chile to all people of good will who wish to know about it. It is because Protestantism means the spiritual orientation of a considerable number of christians in this country. It is a fact that the Protestant Movement in Chile has increased at a greater rhythm than in any other country in Latin America.(5)
>
> It can be said that David Trumbull was the first Protestant missionary who established the first permanent work in Chile, and had a great influence on the historical events of the times.(6)
>
> I venture to assert that the first explanation of the success of Protestantism in Chile is the thirst for God. . . The soul of the Chilean is essentially religious, but it has not been nourished. It is like a fertile field which waits for the planting of the seeds, or has not been adequately cultivated so that the seed might be able to properly bring forth abundant fruit.(7)

In the light of Father Vergara's appraisal of Protestantism in Chile and the use of his symbolism of souls and soils and seeds, the words of David Trumbull were prophetic when, at the end of his Seminary studies and in response to the call from the Foreign Evangelical Society he wrote:

> It seems as though a field was opened there and in some respects as though I am fitted to enter and till it, and scattering seed, to wait patiently for God to give the increase.(8)

Finally, in the 1940's there emerged in Chile amongst the sons of conservative Catholic congressmen, a movement which was inspired by the ideology of the French philosopher, Jacques Maritan. In the 1960's this movement became the Christian Democratic political party. The candidate of this party, Eduardo Frei Montalva was elected to the presidency of the Republic in 1964. His definition of the Christian Democracy was stated as follows:

> Christian Democracy implies an organic and coherent concept, inspired in the values and principles of Christian philosophy. It is an equally deep and universal reply, an interpretation of man

and his fate, and, as a reflection of it, a concept of the human personality that cannot be based on money, class, or race.

The central tenet of Christian Democracy is the belief that we are witnessing to the crisis of a world exhausted to the death of paternalism, and to the birth of a civilization of work and solidarity with man as its center rather than the pursuit of monetary gain that has pervaded the bourgeois society.

In Latin America there is need for a true revolution. Indeed it is already in ferment, but the revolution must take place in freedom.(9)

The success of the Christian Democratic Party in Chile is considered by many political scientists as the only alternative to the frustrations of the ideologies of both the Right and the Left. In fact its emergence and achievements are deemed unique in the Western hemisphere. When it is recalled that David Trumbull's mission and message stressed the same Christian ideology of the freedom and dignity of man and the emancipation of the Chilean Nation-State, it can be said that the Christian Democratic Movement emerged long before the 1940's.

The "Revolution in Freedom" which characterized the Christian Democratic regime of the 1960's served as a preface in the 1970's for a Marxist-Coalition government under the presidency of Dr. Salvador Allende. Much concern was expressed in Chile and abroad, fearing that the country would suffer all the evils of a totalitarian dictatorship. President Allende however reiterated the meaning of his Marxism as a type of Socialism which would best resolve the age-long socio-economic and cultural problems of the nation. What he meant by his political philosophy was best expressed by his Ambassador to the United States in the following speech to President Nixon:

> There is no doubt that many nations in the world are searching today, through different ways, for an answer to the challenge of incorporating increasingly large sectors of their people to responsibilities of government and to the full benefits of development, technology, and civilization. . . As you know, Chile is a country that prides herself of her liberty, of her respect for all philosophical and political doctrines. . . .Mainly based upon those principles, as well as on the Constitution and on the laws that rule our institutional life, the people of Chile have recently chosen a new road which leads to a socialism of their own.

The application of these political doctrines to the Chilean Society appears to have assuaged, for the time being, the earlier forebodings. The Catholic Hierarchy and the lower

Epilogue 117

clergy, Protestant missionaries and Churches have publicly expressed their confidence in the overall administration of the new government. The Embassy of Chile in Washington D. C. reported in its News of March 2, 1971 the following dispatch:

> Dr. Eugene Carson, from the USA, Secretary General of the World Council of Churches, made a statement last week in Geneva, after having met in Santiago with President Allende, saying that he sees 'the Chilean experiment in Socialism as a stimulating and hopeful sign for many countries that share similar difficulties and hopes.' . . .The statement also says that the leaders of the seventeen Protestant Churches told secretary Carson that the new situation in Chile 'is a challenge to find more relevant ways to serve the Gospel and more meaningful ways to witness to it.'

Judging from the dispatches from Geneva and from Santiago it would seem that the Chilean social experiment and the ideology of the 16th century Reformation have much in common.

Appendices

A
ANCESTRAL GOSSIP

Excerpts from a Sketch of the Life of David Trumbull by his son William Trumbull, written in 1925.

David Trumbull came into the world, appropriately enough, on All Saints Day, November 1, 1819, at Elizabeth, New Jersey.

On his mother's side he was Dutch-Scotch. This meant iron in his blood from brave little Holland, iron in his blood from brave little Scotland; it furnished an additional strain of aristocratic breeding destined to prove no mean inheritance for the strenuous life that lay before him. His mother, Hannah Wallace Tunis was of patroon descent, from the Van Teunis stock of Staten Island and New Jersey. Her grandmother, Hannah Wallace, traced her lineage through a clan long prominent in Scottish history. Hannah Tunis died young, at the age of twenty-three, before her son had reached his fourth year, so the lad was left largely in the care of his maternal grandmother, a grim old lady who believed in the rod and used it with fervor as her bounden religious duty.

On one occasion his father, easy-going country gentleman that he was, slipping through life as smoothly as possible, avoiding all its unpleasant responsibilities when he could, sent him with a sealed note to his grandmother in which he asked her to give the boy a sound thrashing for some peccadillo committed in the family circle. The road led to a bridge across a stream, and here the devil

tempted him. Suspecting though not actually knowing what
was in the letter, he dropped it into the stream and watched it float away with mingled feelings of fear and exulta-
tion. The double whaling however, from grandma's formidable arm which promptly followed her learning the facts of
the case, admitted no admixture of feelings. That painful
sequel brought its lasting, salutary lesson.

   At Elizabeth, David attended private school taught by
another stern disciplinarian, one Holtz by name. When
recess hour arrived the street gamins would collect outside, chanting in derisive unison:
        "Holtz's hogs are in the pen;
        They don't get out but now and then:
        When they get out they run about
        ---And then they have to go in again."
This hoodlum taunt of course proved the immediate signal
for a general free fight. A repetition and forerunner,
the glorious melee that followed, of the age-long war between town and gown that has prevailed in the world ever
since boys first learned to go to school. Holtz's insti-
tution, as in the case of Tom Brown at Rugby, turned out
to be a famous school for developing manliness.

   (His father married three times. David was the only
surviving child of the second marriage; two others, both
of them sisters, dying at an early age, one in infancy,
the other at seven.)

   His father's first wife Anne Gibbons was the daughter
of Thomas Gibbons of Savannah and New York, who started a
steamship line in rivalry with Robert Fulton. The latter
had succeeded in securing from the State of New York the
exclusive right to navigate its waters by steam. This
concession Gibbons fought straight up to the Supreme Court
in Washington, claiming that tidewaters around New York
City were solely within the Admiralty or Federal jurisdic-
tion; hence that no such exclusive right could be lawfully
granted by the State. The famous case of Gibbons v Ogden
settled the question definitely in Gibbons favor.

   "When the rivalry between the two steamship lines was
at its height Gibbons frequently traveled on his own boats
running over to Elizabethport. On one occasion his vessel
was held up by fog which was so thick that nothing could
be seen. While chafing and fuming about the delay Gibbons
suddenly heard an oysterman dredging.
"Can you steer us out of this," he called.
"I can steer you out of hell if you want."
He came on board and steered the vessel safely to port.
Gibbons was so delighted with him that he immediately
offered him a position on one of his boats as pilot. The
man was Cornelius Vanderbilt."

Ancestral Gossip

On his father's side David Trumbull came of good old fighting stock. He never could have lived his life without some warrior strain in his blood to lend tonic strength to his character.

During the fifteenth and sixteenth centuries the borderland between England and Scotland was harried by a headstrong, turbulent clan according to the Latin archives of the Heral's office at Edinburgh, claimed descent from a field hand, one William, savior of King Robert Bruce's life in the early days of the fourteenth century. While out hunting, the brilliant colors of the king's retinue as they galloped through the forest near Sterling had roused the wrath of a savage bull who charged furiously at the party. It was a general *sauve qui peut*, the courtiers scattering in all directions, leaving the monarch exposed to the full brunt of the beast's attack. Fortunately a young peasant, inured to the hardest kind of work in the fields had seen the king's imminent danger. Rushing up he seized the brute by the horns, dexterously turning his head and holding it there by main force until the retainers, recovering from their panic, rode back and dispatched the bull with their swords.
"What is your name?" asked the monarch of the rustic.
"William."
"Kneel down, William," commanded the king.
Then drawing his sword he smote him lightly therewith on the back.
"Rise up, Sir William Turnbull."

In addition to knighting on the field for heroic action, which in the days of chivalry was considered a special honor, the monarch gave him an estate near Peebles and conferred on him the right to adopt for his coat of arms three bulls' crests with the motto *Fortuna favet audaci*, only stipulating that in the future he should present himself yearly at Court bringing with him a silver arrow in token of fealty to his liege lord and royal master.

As the clan increased in numbers it succeeded in making itself thoroughly feared and hated by the lowland people on both sides of the border for its impartial marauding. Grown too powerful to please the king of Scotland, suffering from a feud with another clan, it became broken and scattered. Its descendants were dispersed throughout the British Isles. One of the family, John, came to America in 1637 and settled in Rowley, Massachusetts. His great-grandson was the fighting Governor of Connecticut Colony during our Revolutionary period, Washington's "Brother Jonathan," who in 1735 had married Faith Robinson (in Duxbury, Massachusetts) direct descendant on her mother's side of John Alden and Priscilla Mullins.

"Brother Jonathan" was sixty-five years old when the seven-year war with England broke out. Of all the governors of the thirteen colonies in revolt he was the only one with sufficient loyalty to his fellow-colonists or with sufficient moral and physical courage to take up arms against the mother-country, thereby incurring the pronounced hostility of the British government of his day which set a price upon his head. The other governors, being all appointees of the Crown, sided with the home authorities and had to be deposed by the colonists in revolution. He was made jailor of some of them; one had been his classmate at Harvard. George Otto Trevelyan in his history "The American Revolution" places this Puritan patriot in a separate class with Washington and Franklin. That is high praise; perhaps too much so. But there seems little doubt that without his indispensible aid in furnishing supplies to the Commander-in-chief during the two first critical years of the conflict the revolutionary movement must inevitably have failed in its early inception. It was his religious fervor for the patriot cause, his self-sacrificing zeal and toil, in an age too much given to political trimmers waiting to see which way the fortunes of war would lean, that largely saved the day. Washington so regarded it, and Washington of all men ought to have known. The governor's four sons aided him in his work. The oldest, Joseph, was commissary general of the Army, Jonathan Jr. was paymaster, David was the assistant-commissary general, and John, the painter, served as aide-de-camp on Washington's staff.

Our hero came down from David who married Sarah Backus of Norwich in 1778, a lineal descendant on her father's side of the Connecticut Huntingtons, and of Christopher Baret, mayor of Boston, England. He was named after his paternal grandfather.

At the age of fifteen David entered a New York business house, living with a family of Quakers. Though unable to accept all the peculiarities of the Friends' doctrine in its application to practical life, he both felt and said in subsequent years that the world would be a far better world if it could absorb and practice the essential beliefs of that religious body. For its members he ever after entertained loving admiration. He felt that they perhaps came nearer to the true spirit of the Master than any other body of so-called Christians.

Meanwhile foreshadowings of the panic of 1837 were upon the country. In 1832 President Jackson had definitely locked horns with the money power of the land by vetoing the new charter of the United States Bank. Three successive mercantile houses in which the lad found employment went to the wall. He decided, as he was wont to say later, that evidently the Lord did not intend him for a business man. This mortality of commercial ventures, however, always exercised his imagination. He had read somewhere that statement of some statistical romancer that over ninety-five per cent of new mercantile undertakings failed; and it often occupied his waking thoughts. While undoubtedly an exaggeration there still remained no gainsaying the fact, depressingly melancholy to a thoughtful mind, that the mortality was frightful, particularly among the "little fellows" of the commercial world. Of business in general he used to say that his experience and observation of life had taught him that while business at times grows very, very sick it never dies.

At this juncture relatives of his mother in Baltimore decided to practically adopt him, and he was invited to come and make his permanent home with them. But on the very night of his arrival his host, husband of his cousin, went suddenly out of his head, and coming into the young boy's room with a loaded pistol he fired at some supposed enemy, the bullet lodging in the wall right over the lad's head.

Next day while on his way home by boat he got to thinking pretty seriously about the dark things of life. Here indeed was food for thought for an impressionable, adolescent mentality. On the one hand the mystery of insanity, sudden like a bolt from the blue: What did it mean? On the other, the mystery of death, or an escape therefrom so narrow as to make his preservation appear all the more miraculous: again what did it mean? The way of it kept forcing itself upon his soul. Saul's lightning flash on the road to Damascus had been re-enacted in different form. Once more he decided, as he used to say later, that God must have spared his life to some purpose. It must be college for him; a teacher's career; possibly the seminary.

There was in those days a famous Bacon Academy at Colchester in Connecticut, where his father had recently settled on account of its educational advantages. Here he betook himself and so came under the influence of Rev. Mr. Arnold, idealist, one of the profoundly formative forces in his life which helped to definitely settle his resolution and crystallize his decision on the ministry. He was always proud of his profession. To be an ambassador of God, he maintained was, if rightly understood, a far higher honor than that of ambassador of any earthly potentate. And as regards its possibilities for lasting good, who could measure the power of suggestion emanating from one sane idealist's life?

His father used to laugh at his scholastic ambitions. "Humph, Dave," the pater would say, "I've forgotten more Latin than you'll ever know." But he pegged away at his studies and when he went down to Yale found himself advanced enough to enter the sophomore Class of 1842.

Spain has a grim old proverb, *la letra entra con sangre y fuego*, or "the knowledge of letters enters through blood and fire." This may serve fairly well to paint the hardships of college life at that time. Compulsory chapel at half past five in the morning during fall and spring terms, at half past six in winter, and every evening as well; no heat in the dormitories save from wood fires; chilblains so common that it was the customary thing to dash out of old South Middle and stand barefoot in the snow on the campus so as to get a few minutes relief from burning feet; ice forming regularly in bedroom pitchers and having to be broken before the early morning wash; wretched food in College Commons, so meagre, so bad, that it led later to the famous bread and butter rebellion. But why go on? Who cared so long as one could be a member of "Linonia" or "Brothers in Unity" and spout oracular orations to an age that took itself delightfully seriously, or which made at least a gallant pretense of doing so.

The three years at Princeton Seminary from 1842-1845 brought him under the influence of another rare spirit, that of Professor Alexander, which was also destined to have a prodound effect upon his character and life. Meanwhile pioneer work in some out-lying portion of the globe appealed strongly to his soul. Toward the close of his seminary course Dr. Alexander came to him one day and spoke of an opening in far-off Valparaiso, Chile, to labor among the seamen and at the same time build up an English-speaking church in that lonely, windy outpost of civilization. Would he accept?

Sailors at that time were an absolutely neglected class of society. They felt that no one cared anything about them. They thought that landsmen considered them too worthless to be noticed. As a natural consequence they gave themselves up when ashore to reckless dissipation in drinking hells and brothels where they were preyed upon by harpies who gouged them out of their last penny. Dr. Ashley in England had made a gallant attempt at rescue in 1836 with his first Mission Ship in the Bristol Channel, and the movement was being copied in America. But beyond this little or nothing had been done for our sailor lads in any of the great world seaports.

Journeying to Valparaiso in the days of sailing ships often meant a six-months voyage around Cape Horn, that ancient terror and haunting nightmare of all mariners. David sailed from Baltimore in July 1845, having incidentally saved the life of a young girl from drowning in the waters of the bay. His children later in life were wont to quiz him about this romantic affair asking why he had not kept track of the young lady and whether "she might not have come within a shaving of being their mother," if he had only done so. But he never vouchsafed any further particulars. To dwell upon details I suppose would have struck him as boasting. The bare fact of the rescue was enough. Meanwhile a good-humored chuckle at their romantic foolishness and curiosity proved their only reward. It had all lain in the day's work.

He used to joke over the reminiscence that just prior to sailing he was approached by an enterprising real-estate agent who offered to sell him some choice lots in a small town then growing rapidly on the south west shore of Lake Michigan. The city had been incorporated only eight years before, and stood around the site of old Fort Dearborn; but it promised well as an investment. Not being overburdened with cash, and needing what little he had for unforeseen contingencies in his South American mission, he was obliged to forego the tempting opportunity. When he saw Chicago thirty years later on the occasion of one of his visits to the United States, he received ocular proof of the difference in rate of growth between the cities of North and South America.

While at Princeton he had studied Spanish. On the long voyage out he was asked by his fellow passengers (there were some dozen on board interested for the most part in mercantile pursuits), to give them lessons. He set for them to translate the simple phrase, "I will love," and they went to work with a will, boning and laboring over their dictionaries; but with startling results. "*Yo voluntad amor*," was the best their combined efforts could produce.

The long voyage led past the Sargasso sea and the doldrums around the Equator, included fighting the baffling winds off the Horn for weary weeks, winds that would sometimes sweep the vessel back in twenty-four hours to the identical spot where it had stood many days before. The ship's skipper was a reckless devil who believed in crowding on all possible sail no matter what the weather. In the North and South Atlantic where vessels are apt to be taken suddenly aback by unexpected shifts in the wind, this often proved a very dangerous hazard. It is true those were the days when the clipper ship era had just about commenced and our Yankee captains were not averse to taking chances. But the slow going *Mississippi* on which David traveled was not a clipper ship. She failed to make

Valparaiso harbor before Christmas Day, six months out from Baltimore. On her next voyage the vessel was lost. She disappeared utterly off the face of the waters and was never heard from again, probably capsized by a sudden squall while carrying too much sail.

B

A SEAMAN'S FRIEND

Excerpt from "My Saga" by Anita Trumbull Atwater.

Characters in the story as retold:

Abuelita - Grandmother Jane Fitch Trumbull
Meetoo   - (me-too) Julia Trumbull-Dodge
Tinini   - (from the Spanish "Tia" plus Anita)
Chico   - Anita's younger brother William who was much taller than she

We children felt there was a chance for a story. We began an attack and gave Meetoo no mercy.

"Today in Dieziocho," she began, "the 18th of September, children, the day Chile won her independence. So listen well and remember this story grows from a seed that was really a pearl, and is the one I love best.

Tinini and I were girls at Wellesley College, too far from Valparaiso to go home for vacation.

Luckily, something always happened to find favor for us. One summer morning on Nantucket Island we were invited to join a tally-ho picnic -- a top-heavy coach pulled by six horses, the two nearest the wheels trotting in the footsteps of those in the lead."

Already we had begun to see ourselves. There was such charm in the story, I pulled Chico down to keep him quiet.

"Across a misty moor we set off for Sankaty Head Lighthouse. To let people know we were coming, the coach-driver blew a ran-tan-ta-ra on a silver trumpet. 'This is something I like, driving six up,' he said, holding six reins well in one hand.

He bustled with his own importance. Imposing as a Roman charioteer, he wore a fine blue coat, a cocked hat crowned with a feather that turned with the wind, his trousers were of home-spun something or other, a red cravat was fastened with a silver horseshoe, and silver buckles on his vast boots planted on the dashboard.

A post-rider astride the off-wheel horse puffed himself up in a hurry to leave the miles behind him. The noise and color started sheep on the run. Partridges and larks rose, rabbits and a lonely deer ran away into hedges of honeysuckle and bayberry.

The morning was as blue as a Chilean sky. One cloud balancing above reminded us of South America.

Nantucket, a friendly neighborly island! We girls were sure of that when we saw *Valparaiso* painted on the blue door of a gray cottage.

No longer foreigners, Tinini pulled on the driver's coattails. "I'll give you anything if you stop and let us find out why the name of our home is painted on that door," she said, standing up to jump.

"Never do that again, young lady," the driver growled angrily, "but this time I'll allow you. Whoa, whoo-up boys and girls," he shouted out and skidded in such a hurry he just about fell off his perch.

If he had refused, there wouldn't be any story. The horses dragged to a standstill.

We straddled over him and climbed down over high wheels. We stopped. Heaven knows we stopped, and nearly broke up the party.

Hand in hand, we two unlatched a wicket gate and walked up a shell path, past sweet briar roses, lobster traps and fish nets drying.

A dog barked.

"Good mornin', young ladies," said an old sea-faring man, looking up from boat gear he mended. Every where around was the flavor of tar and salt water. A northeaster beard like a lion's mane went all around his face. Smoke from his pipe curled up into an apple tree.

"Good morning, sir. We are just wondering about 'Valparaiso'".

"Come on. Don't mind old Hinge. He sort of breaks the ice round here. Gentle as a lamb he is -- he is."

"Forgive us for trespassing, sir. We are two girls from Chile. Valparaiso is our home, and we didn't mean to disturb you."

"Well, most folks adorn their domiciles with names they want to remember, don't they? This here is my home. Won't you two sit a while and tell me your names? I'm a sailor, I am."

We had forgotten the tallyho. There was no doubt they had forgotten us. We couldn't suppress curiosity much longer. We smelled the inviting small of bread baking. A grasshopper sang under a morning-glory vine.

A door opened from the cottage, and a tall, slender woman in a blue gingham dress made a little voyage down the path to bring a chip basket of raspberries. "They're fresh-picked. Won't you girls enjoy them? Father's astonished, I can see, but he never lets you know, unless he says so," she said ever so kindly.

"Young ladies, my name is Nathaniel Tozzer, and Mrs. Perley Davis here is my one and only daughter -- she is -- she is. . . Well, let me tell you all a far away, long ago story. Search me, daughter, a man can't help havin' memories. Make your minds easy, everybody. I'll entertain you girls to the best of my ability. Beats all. I don't believe half the yarns I tell, but this one's goin' to be pure gospel, gold and glory, if I do say so myself. Come on, we're goin' on a spree. Too good to be true. Pure gospel, gold and glory!"

He seemed to swell up a little and looked all around to make sure of his house and garden. "There was a time when all of New England was too small for your humble servant. Bein' clipperborn, I scampered off from New Bedford on a lame duck to discover the world unknown. I just tied my nest egg up in knots and started out to be a pirate over the rollin' sea. And nary a notion where she was goin' to.

"In no time at all, at all, I'd had enough common calamity, reef and furl, eppidemicks and dyin'. Don't ask me to abumbrate the life I lived, polishin' off those hellimonious Ramarees round the Forge of Storms. The confounded cold froze us all day -- all night. Rotten riggin', cracked masts. Touch and go. The sun was high at midnight -- the moon at crack of noon.

"Miserable boy, I'd have left the sea forever, only the more days, the more dollars. Nothing to say about this day or that day, except pay waited at Talcaguano -- good Chilean pesos, English pounds, American dollars, and things would be hunky-dory. Well, still a-float, we reached Valpo.

"Nothin' to see to larboard but high mountains, and to leeward the same eternal ocean to land us past the golden gate in Russian America.

"I must have been somewhere between fifteen and twenty: hard-up years wantin' to play the man you're goin' to be. Well, I wasn't in the money business, and in Hell's kitchen they sheared me of every scurrilous red cent, without a livin' soul to say a word for my fallen fortune in any language I could say at all, at all.

"Just to show how the wind tempers to a shorn lamb, there I was huntin' for a place to hide. Loath to tell, I carried more sail then ballast next morin'. All my bearin's lost -- not an inch of towrope and nary a breeze.

"Triflin' away time in a wrecked world, I heard an animal comin' downhill. A man horseback stopped alongside. He reached a hand down and scared me in a conniption fit, thinkin' he wanted to get me up there in the saddle.

"So far, Valpo hadn't been any good, but then my notion of despair moved off.

"'My boy, you just took hold of the poker by the wrong end,' he said in good old New Bedford talk. "That's all," -- and I reached up for a card he gave me.

"Who can say what a lonesome jack-tar picks up when there's nothin' to do? Next thing, so far from my folks, black smallpox got me. Somehow, I didn't yearn to die all by myself. I couldn't go back to the sea again, and I didn't even try to look any braver than I felt. Bear with me, ladies. Poison blisters and all, I looked him up. He never took me for a mendacious beggar cravin' charity. He just took my arm and hauled me inside his house.

"I'll never know what bawdy words I said, cursin' in deliriums. They never thought of them; then, after they saved my life, they gave me a chance to be a kind of handyman around, till they just freed me from every last one of those hallucinations -- him and the Missus, as gentle a lady-angel as ever comforted a footloose boy who didn't even know what town he was in.

"I never was one to be bitten by the serpent's tooth of ingratitude, but what could I do now? I didn't have anything in the world but a solitary pearl -- a black one, to sell maybe; then, thinking it over, and emboldened just because she was so friendly, I apologized and gave her my pearl. 'You're welcome to it for taking the chips off my shoulders and everything,' I said, kind of distracted because it was the best thing I ever did. 'I'm just tryin' to say goodbye with thanks,' -- and she took hold of my hand and answered, 'Always I've wanted something as lovely.'

"This was a kind of omen. They changed the whole course of my future life. He gave me a suit of clothes with fifty pesos in a pocket, and he put me on a vessel bound for New Bedford. 'Don't thank me,' he said. 'Just keep in mind you helped me by letting me help you.'

"Young ladies, all my life till I swallowed the anchor, roughly speakin' -- that's why Valparaiso's painted on my door. My home, after travellin' round the world fifty times to find it. That town is just like it sounds -- a Valley of Paradise."

Tinini and I looked at each other. It all linked up like summer lightning with great tales of the sea and ships. There was Jonah and the whale, Noah's ark, and Tobit, the angel, the miraculous wedding feast, the blind man healed of his blindness, and the famous fish, the Skeleton in Armor, not to tell of many others.

"Oh, Mr. Tozzer, we don't need to ask. Just tell us if the name on the card was *David Trumbull*? Father had your pearl set in flowery gold, and Mother calls it 'Columbia the Gem of the Ocean. My goodness, nothing is too good to be true!" we said, interrupting each other and talking at the same time.

"Jumpin' Johoshophat! I want to know! I wouldn't belittle it. You take my word for it, and I'll take yours."

Just then, the tallyho driver blew a despairing note that scared us.

"Great snakes! Tell that high-falutin' monkey to stop tootin' tra-la-la. You girls just take it from an old wind-jammer friend of the Trumbulls -- the mills of the Gods grind show, but exceedin' sure."

We had eaten all the raspberries. Mrs. Davis said she better get started white-washing the stems of her apple trees. "Now, you girls promise, if you ever come joy-riding again, be sure to come see us."

How Meetoo traced the end of the story is lost in many tellings. Stories that may seem trivial, but it transformed the world to know there were people like that.

All our born days, Abuelita, Tinini, Meetoo and I have fanned flames of enthusiasm for Chile by singing their songs and telling their stories.

C

LETTERS WRITTEN BY DAVID TRUMBULL

To His Sister Caroline

New Haven, August 4th, 1840

Dear Sister Caroline.

   I often think of you, and have wished to receive a letter from you during this term, but none has arrived as yet, so I embrace this opportunity to send you a short note. I should like to know how you progress in your studies, what you are reading, how you pass your time and all such matters as your brother would feel an interest in; also more than all I should like to know your religious feelings, whether you are going forward or backward, I say more than all because if your religious feelings be as they ought every thing else will be right. You must not be satisfied with present or past feelings, piety *must live* every day or it is not piety; strive to have your "path brighter and brighter unto the perfect day." It is in your power to attain too high degree of piety, then be satisfied with no mean amount of love to *God* -- but love him with all the heart, think on his character and study his word. Bring your religion into all you do, whether great or small -- act thinking that God sees you, even your thoughts, and *often* ask yourself does God approve of what I am doing? Never say I can do this or neglect because others act so, but make *duty* the motto of life. You are the eldest at home save John and it is incumbent on you to show the younger members that there is truth in religion besides the name, and let your influence at home be in favor of piety all the time -- you can cause a great deal of happiness then if you will pursue the right course yourself -- self denial and kindness toward everybody, is the secret of a pleasant life.

Well now goodbye I can write no more.
Your affectionate brother -- David.

P.S. In your prayers *never forget* your inpenitent brothers -- their prospect is awful unless they repent.

To Edward Law Baldwin Esq.
(Edward Law Baldwin was son of Governor Rodger S. Baldwin and was a classmate of David Trumbull at Yale College in 1842.)

Colchester, Conn.,
July 8, 1845,

Edward Law Baldwin Esq.,
2 Hannover St., New York.

Dear Sir:

Accept my sincere thanks for taking the pains to procure and send to me the valuable letter of introduction from your father to Admiral Wooster. I shall feel much grateful in presenting it.

It would have been agreeable to have remained longer in Hartford till it was ready, but having been away from home for a year, and a prospect of still a longer absence, I was bound to hurry on.

My father said at the arrival of the letter he had voted for Governor Baldwin twice, when he knew nothing about him more than being a candidate. Hereafter he should vote for him by all means, for he felt acquainted with him. And now as perhaps I may not again meet you, farwell -- I am sure I wish you the very best success in your path of life: and hope you will not think it obtrusion, if I urge on paper, that I have so poorly urged in example, the need you have of attention to the inner wants of the Soul, which are bound up in its relation to God the Great Judge: since we have all ofended Him it cannot be wise to neglect the offer of Reconciliation made in the Gospel -- that offer I hope and pray, you my friend, may be able to appreciate and accept.

Very sincerely your friend,

David Trumbull

To Yale President Theodore Dwight Woolsey

Brooklyn, New York,
November 20, 1866.

Reverend President Woolsey, D.D.,
New Haven, Connecticut.

Replying to your note about the Bible Society we have enough copies of the Scriptures but other publications are necessary -- some to disabuse the minds of men who have been prejudiced against the reading of the Bible, or who are skeptical -- also to awaken attention and consent to the Cross.

In addition to the generous supply of the Bible Society there is need of attractive christian polemical literature (in love speaking the truth) didactic, apologetic and narrative.

The Bible is the standard of appeal, but we must make our appeals to it. The few articles I have prepared and published in Chile have drawn attention to the Scriptures and facilitate their sale. On this continent there are twenty million who need Evangelical Christian doctrine and are accessible.

Yours sincerely,

David Trumbull

NOTES

CHAPTER 1. *The New England Heritage*

1. *The History and Character of Calvinism*, p. 436.
2. Perry Miller and Thomas H. Johnson, (eds.) 2 vols., *The Puritans*, I.p.1.
3. Ralph Barton Perry, *Puritanism and Democracy*, pp. 195-196.
4. Louise L. Green, *The Development of Religious Liberty in America*, pp. 495-496.
5. *Connecticut State Register and Manual*, Hartford: State of Connecticut, 1967, p. 41.
6. *Ibid.*, p. 23.
7. Williston Walker, *A History of the Christian Church*, Revised ed. 1969, pp. 507-508.
8. Fred Field Goodsell, *You Shall be my Witness*, pp. 34 and 99. See also by the same author, *They Lived Their Faith*, p. 44.
9. Henry Otis Dwight, *The Centennial History of the American Bible Society*, pp. 146-147.
10. *Constitution of the American Tract Society*, New York, 1825.
11. American Seamen's Friend Society, *First Annual Report*, May 1829, p. 17.
12. *The Christian World*, "Historical Sketch of the Work of the American and Foreign Christian Union", March, 1883, p. 1.

CHAPTER 2. *Family Portrait*

1. John Trumbull, *Autobiography: Reminiscences and Letters*, Revised ed. by Theodor Sizer, 1953, (New Haven: Yale University Press), pp. 1-3.
2. J. Hammond Trumbull (ed.), *The Memorial History of Hartford County, Connecticut 1633-1884*, p. 410.
3. The middle name "Mason" was used to distinguish him from other John Trumbulls in the genealogy.
4. As a young entrepreneur, he borrowed funds from his uncle Col. John Trumbull in order to carry on an export-import trade with the West Indies and China, during the years 1824-25.
5. Rev. Edwin F. Hatfield, *History of Elizabeth Town, New Jersey*, Cornelius Vanderbilt was a pilot of this line and this was the beginning of his millions.
6. William Hall, The Old Homes-"Cherry Lawn", The Elizabeth Daily Journal, July 15, 1873.
7. For information concerning the births and deaths of the family see *The Record Book of the First Presbyterian Church* of Elizabeth, New Jersey, 1688-1966, and *Inscriptions on the Tombstones in the Burial Ground of the First Presbyterian Church 1664-1892*.
8. David Trumbull, Journal, November (no day) 1842.
9. The Record Book of the First Presbyterian Church of Elizabethtown, p. xix.
10. *Ibid*.
11. Yale College, Class of 1842, Biographical Record of the Class of 1842, New Haven, 1878, p. 194.
12. *The Record*, Vol. 18, No. 291, Valparaiso, February 23, 1889.
13. Biographical Record, *Op.Cit.*, p. 195.
14. William E. Dodge, *The Record*, *Op.Cit.*, February 23, 1889, p. 10.
15. Personal interview with Mrs. Hester T. Standish II, granddaughter of David Trumbull.
16. Roland H. Bainton, "Manuscript, "Student Life under the Elms and Over the Sea."
17. *Ibid*.
18. *Ibid.*, p. 10.
19. Private Journal of Jane Wales Fitch, October 5, 1848, New Haven. The Journals are in the keeping of Miss Alice Trumbull of Santiago, Chile.
20. *Ibid*.
21. Interview with Mrs. Claire Trumbull Higgins.
22. Quoted from Robert E. Speer, *Studies of Missionary Leadership*, p. 228.
23. Yale University, Biographies of Graduates, pp. 186-187.

24. The Baltimore Affair refers to the incident when the Secretary of State of the United States demanded a gun salute to the North American flag and also indemnity for the U. S. sailors who were killed in a brawl in the port of Valparaiso, Chile. See Hubert Herring's *A History of Latin America*, p. 557.
25. John Trumbull, MD., Andean Melodies, pp. 4, 10, 43, 58, 61, 79, 80, 82, and 84.
26. Yale College, *Biographies of Graduates, History of the Class of 1880*, pp. 262-264. See also *The Record*, No. 177, August 28, 1884, Vol. 13, p. 6.
27. David Trumbull, Journal and Prayer Notes, December, 1878.
28. *The Record*, Vol. 18, No. 291, Valparaiso, February 23, 1889, p. 14.
29. *Ibid.*, November 18, 1887, p. 15, and December 16, 1887, p. 14.
30. Yale College, Biographical Sketches of Graduate Members, pp. 236-238.
31. From his dossier, Yale College, Richard Lindsay Trumbull.
32. Anita T. Atwater, *My Saga*. An unpublished story of her life, 2 vols., 1960, Chapter I, p. 9. See the Appendix for the story as told by Julia Trumbull.
33. *Ibid.*, Chapter V, pp. 26-32.

CHAPTER 3. *The Education and Call to Service of David Trumbull*

1. p. xl and p. 3.
2. p. 1 and p. 12.
3. A letter from David Trumbull to William E. Shenck, D.D., written at Valparaiso, January 3, 1878.
4. George P. Fisher, *Life of Benjamin Silliman*, Vol. I, pp. 231-232.
5. Yale University, Class Letter, 1888.
6. *Ibid.*
7. Sidney E. Mead, *The Lively Experiment*, p. 123. Also see Curtis Manning Geer, *The Hartford Theological Seminary*, "The Taylor-Tyler Controversy", Chapter II and Stokes,   , p. 67.
8. Quotes from the Journal of David Trumbull, November 1, 1840, November 8, 1840, March 14, 1841.
9. Stokes, *Op.Cit.*, p. 14
10. Fred Field Goodsell, *You Shall be My Witnesses*, p. 8.
11. Ebenezer C. Tracy, Memoir of the Life of Jeremiah Evarts, Esq., p. 426, (quoted from Robert E. Speer, Studies of Missionary Leadership, p. 62-63).
12. Fred Field Goodsell, *They Lived Their Faith*, pp. 201-203, and Bainton, *Op.Cit.*, pp. 192-196.

Notes 141

13. Stokes, *Op.Cit.*, p. 92.
14. David Trumbull, *The Record*, May 1887, "Yale in the Olden Times, p. 11.
15. William L. Kingsley, *The New Englander and Yale Review*, June, 1899.
16. Alexander A. Hodge, *Life of Charles Hodge*, p. 287. (These heresies had to do with the imputation of original sin and the freedom and responsibility of man in the plan of salvation.)
17. David Trumbull, Journal, September 18, 1842.
18. *Ibid.*
19. *Ibid.*, February 6, 1845.
20. Hodge, *Op.Cit.*, 258-259.
21. *Ibid.*, p. 457.
22. *Ibid.*, pp. 340-342, and p. 613.
23. *Ibid.*, p. 384.
24. David Trumbull, Letter to Professor W. Henry Green, March 18, 1872, and a reply to a circular letter from Rev. William E. Schenck, Alumni Secretary, Princeton Theological Seminary.

CHAPTER 4. *Forerunners in the Vale of Paradise*

1. Eusebio Lillo, author of the Chilean National Anthem.
2. Conquistador Francisco Pizarro founded the city of Lima, Peru on January 6, 1535. He called it "The City of the Kings" in honor of the visit of the magi who came to adore the Christ-child the 6th of January.
3. From the letter sent by the Conquistador of Chile: Don Pedro de Valdivia to His Majesty King Charles V, the 4th of September, 1545. These words are engraved on a large stone in the central park of the capital city Santiago, called "Cerro Santa Lucia."
4. Ricardo Donoso, *Las Ideas Políticas en Chile* (The Political Ideas in Chile), p. 177.
5. *Ibid.*, p. 98.
6. William Rex Crawford, *A Century of Latin American Thought*, p. 61.
7. Armando Donoso, *El Evangelio Americano y Paginas Selectas*, p. 7.
8. Armando Donoso, *The Dynamic Ideas of Francisco Bilbao*, 6th Ed., p. 12-13.
9. Kenneth Scott Latourette, *Christianity in a Revolutionary Age*, Vol. I, p. 402.
10. *Op.Cit.*, p. 23.
11. *Op.Cit.*, pp. 113-120.
12. Francisco Bilbao, *El Evangelio Americano y Paginas Selectas* (The American Gospel and Selected Writings), p. 13.

13. Eugenio Pereira Salas, *Henry Hill: Merchant, Vice-Consul and Missionary*, pp. 5-6.
14. Henry Hill, *Recollections of an Octogenarian*, pp. 145-150.
15. *Ibid.*, pp. 191 ff.
16. *Missionary Herald*, Vol. XIX, February 1823, p. 56.
17. *Op. Cit.*, p. 27.
18. Domingo Amunategui Solar, *El Sistema Lancaster en Chile y en Otros Paises Sud-Americanos* (The Lancaster System in Chile and Other Countries in South America), pp. 147-148.
19. *Ibid.*, p. 28.
20. Webster E. Browning, *Joseph Lancaster, James Thompson and the Lancastrian System of Mutual Instruction with Special Reference to Latin America*, pp. 27-28.
21. Amunátegui Solar, *Op. Cit.*, pp. 160-161.
22. *Ibid.*, 129-130.
23. *Ibid.*, p. 326.
24. William Adams, *Life and Service of Rev. John C. Brigham*.
25. J. Orlin Oliphant, "The Parvin-Brigham Mission to Spanish America, 1823-1826," *Church History*, Vol. xix, pp. 82-103.
26. *Ibid.*, p. 91.
27. H. O. Dwight, *Centenial History of the American Bible Society*, pp. 180-181.
28. *Missionary Herald*, Vol. XXII, No. 10, October 26, p. 297.
29. *Missionary Herald*, Vol. XXII, October-November 1826, p. 343.
30. *Ibid.*, p. 341.
31. J. Orin Oliphant, *Op. Cit.*, pp. 102-103.
32. David Trumbull, *The Christian World*, July 1866, p. 211.
33. J. B. Alberdi, *Life of William Wheelwright in South America*, p. 212.
34. *Ibid.*, pp. 205-206.
35. *Ibid.*, p. 41.
36. *Ibid.*, p. 5 of the Appendix.
37. *Ibid.*, pp. 163-164.
38. David Trumbull, *The Record*, November 15, 1873, p. 45.
39. Alberdi, *Op. Cit.*, Appendix, p. 8.
40. American Bible Society, *Agents in Partibus*, 1832-1841, pp. 146-147.
41. Charles F. Hillman (Quien Sabe), *Old Timers, British and North American in Chile*, p. 150 ff. and Alberdi, *Op. Cit.*, p. 205.
42. *Dictionary of American Biographies*, Vol. XX, pp. 63-64.

Notes   143

CHAPTER 5. *The Reformed Church in the Wilderness*

1. W. E. Dodge, *The Record*, February 23, 1889, p. 11.
2. David Trumbull, Letter to his family, January 1846.
3. David Trumbull, *Sailors' Magazine*, August 1846, p. 378.
4. American Seamens' Friend Society, *19th Annual Report*, May 10, 1847.
5. Ricardo Donoso, *Las Ideas Políticas en Chile* (The Political Ideas in Chile), p. 181.
6. *Ibid.*, pp. 216-217.
7. David Trumbull, *The Record*, "A bimonthly publication edited by David Trumbull," 18 Vols., 1871-1889", November 16, pp. 6-7.
8. *The Christian World*, Vol. XX, No. 10, October 1869, p. 276.
9. James H. McLean, *Historia de la Iglesia Presbiteriana de Chile* (History of Presbyterian Church in Chile), pp. 40-44.
10. *The Christian World*, December 1871, p. 389.
11. David Trumbull, Letter to the Presbyterian Board of Missions, *Chile Letters*, Vol. 32, No. 167.
12. Webster E. Browning, "Education in Chile" from W. Reginald Wheeler, et.al., *Modern Missions in Chile and Brazil*, p. 162.
13. *Christian World*, May, 1867, p. 153.
14. David Trumbull, Letter to The Christian World while he was in the United States, January 1867, p. 24.
15. Arthur Judson Brown, *One Hundred Years*, p. 106.
16. Florence E. Smith, "Some Significant Aspects of the History of the Chile Mission" in *Op. Cit.*, *Modern Missions in Chile and Brazil*, pp. 150-151.
17. F. F. Ellingwood, *The Record*, Letter from Secretary of the Mission Board to David Trumbull, March 22, 1884, p. 3.
18. F. F. Ellingwood, Letter to David Trumbull, June 21, 1884.
19. W. Stanley Rycroft, *The Ecumenical Witness of the United Presbyterian Church in the United States of America*, pp. 216 and 293.

CHAPTER 6. *Agent of the Evangelical Magisterium*

1. Francisco Antonio Encina, *Historia de Chile*, Vol. XI, p. 39.
2. Francisco A. Encina, *Op. Cit.*, Vol. XII, p. 439.
3. Matthew 28:19-20.
4. *Chilean Times*, August 4, 1888.

5. Amanda Labarca, *History of Teaching in Chile*, pp. 200, 215.
6. Ricardo Donoso, *The Political Ideas in Chile*, pp. 220-226.
7. *Ibid.*, p. 315. See also *The Record*, January 5, 1884, p. 8.
8. Oswald Hardey Evans, *The Mackay School: An Outline of its History 1857-1957*. David Trumbull was chairman of this Society for several years, pp. 32 and 78.
9. *Ibid.*, p. 31.
10. *Ibid.*, pp. 12-13.
11. Wallis Hunt, *Heirs of Great Adventure; The History of Balfour Williamson Company*, Limited, Vol. I, p. 12.
12. Oswald Hardey Evans, *Op. Cit.*, p. 37.
13. *Ibid.*, p. 37.
14. *Ibid.*, p. 82.
15. *Ibid.*, pp. 33-34.
16. Francisco A. Encina, *Historia de Chile*, Vol. XIV, p. 17.
17. David Trumbull, *The Record*, April 5, 1884, and *The Christian World*, December 1871, p. 386.
18. Interview with Maximilano Salas-Marchant by the writer, Valparaiso, July 1947.
19. School Paper "Sunshine," November 1938.
20. For a detailed account of the Instituto Inglés read W. R. Wheeler, et.al., *Modern Missions in Chile and Brazil*, pp. 152-165 and 67-74. Also Webster E. Browning, *What the Old Boys Say*, a collection of fifty letters written to Dr. Browning by the alumni.

CHAPTER 7. *The Word of God is Spread Abroad*

1. American Bible Society, *Eighty-First Report*, 1897, pp. 106-107.
2. *Christian World*, February 1860, p. 59.
3. *Ibid.*, p. 59.
4. Williston Walker, *A History of the Christian Church*, p. 378.
5. *Ibid.*, pp. 523-524.
6. Charles F. Hillman, *(Quien Sabe): Old Timers-British and Americans in Chile*, pp. 383-385.
7. Historical Records of the American Bible Society and from a *Vaughan New Testament* in the Society's Library.
8. Hillman, *Loc. Cit.*
9. *The Christian World*, December 1877, pp. 360-361.
10. Wallis Hunt, *Heirs of Great Adventure: The History of Balfour, Williamson and Company Limited*, 1851-1901, pp. 62-63.
11. David Trumbull, *The Record*, March 29, 1879.

12. David Trumbull, Annual Meeting of the Valparaiso Bible Society, 1884, *The Record*, March 6, 1884, pp. 3-4.
13. W. E. Dodge, Annual Meeting of the Valparaiso Bible Society for 1886, *The Record*, March 10, 1887.
14. American Bible Society, *Seventy-sixth Report*, 1892, p. 109.
15. American Bible Society, *Seventy-third Report*, 1889, p. 92.
16. William Canton, *History of the British and Foreign Bible Society*, p. 335.
17. United Bible Societies, *News and Views*, January 26, 1968.

CHAPTER 8. *The Gospel in the Reformed Tradition*

1. John Calvin, *The Institutes of the Christian Religion, III*, pp. xvi and 1.
2. *The Record*, October 21, 1887, p. 3.
3. David Trumbull, *The Record*, March 29, 1879, p. 1.
4. W. E. Dodge, *The Record*, February 23, 1889, p. 15.
5. David Trumbull, *Christian World*, February 1878, *The Union Church in Valparaiso*, and *The Record*, November 25, 1877.
6. *Ibid*.
7. *The Record*, November 18, 1887, *Valdivia; Good News*.
8. *The Record*, January 5, 1884, "The First Protestant Service in Valparaiso," p. 1.
9. *The Record*, July 17, 1884, p. 5.
10. Wallis Hunt, *Heirs of Great Adventure, The History of Balfour, Williamson and Company Limited 1851-1901*, pp. 59-60, 63, and 65.
11. David Trumbull, *The Record*, "Rome or Santiago," December 31, 1884.
12. For the accounts of these Church-State Conflicts see: Luis Galdames, *A History of Chile*, Tr., Isaac Joslin Cox, pp. 338-340; Ricardo Donoso, *Las Ideas Políticas en Chile*; pp. 290-298, and J. Lloyd Mecham, *Church and State in Latin America*, pp. 258-260.
13. *Constitution of the American Tract Society*, Instituted at New York in 1825, Article I.
14. Florence E. Smith, *Modern Missions in Chile and Brazil, The Gospel for the Chileans*, pp. 135-136. In the 1960's Chile suffered a two-year drought causing widespread disaster due to lack of hydroelectrical energy in mining and industry. The government appealed to the United States to dispatch to Chile vessels of appropriate electrical generating capacities to help meet the need of the emergency. (News from the Embassy of Chile 122, July 27, 1968.)

15. Ricardo Donoso, *Las Ideas Políticas en Chile*, pp. 174-175.
16. Roland H. Bainton, *Yale and the Ministry*, "The Temperance Campaign," pp. 136-141. The Connecticut Temperance Society was formed in 1829 with Jeremiah Day of Yale College as president. *Ibid.*, p. 138.
17. *The Record*, November 19, 1884, p. 9, and May 19, 1887, p. 6.
18. Charles F. Hillman (Quien Sabe) *"Old Timers" British and American, in Chile*, pp. 277-270.
19. Hubert Herring, *A History of Latin America: From the Beginning to the Present*, p. 589.
20. Frederick B. Pike, *United States, 1880-1962: The Emergence of Chile's Social Crisis and the Challenge to the United States Diplomacy*, pp. 277-278.

CHAPTER 9. *Advocate of Constitutional Reforms*

1. William Miller Collier and Guillermo Feliu Cruz, *La Primera Mision de Los Estados Unidos de America en Chile*, pp. 109-110.
2. Ricardo Donoso, *Las Ideas Políticas en Chile*, p. 181.
3. Luis Galdames, *A History of Chile*, Tr., Isaac Joslin Cox, pp. 338-339.
4. *The Christian World*, March 1877, p. 87.
5. Henry Clay Evans, Jr., *Chile and Its Relation with the United States*, pp. 71-72.
6. Ricardo Donoso, *Las Ideas Políticas en Chile*, p. 236.
7. Maria Graham, *Diary of a Residence in Chile*, pp. 207-208.
8. Donoso, *Op. Cit.*, p. 240.
9. James H. McLean, *Historia de la Iglesia Presbiteriana en Chile* (History of the Presbyterian Church in Chile), pp. 23-24.
10. Donoso, *Op. Cit.*, pp. 259-283.
11. Luis Galdames, *History of Chile*, pp. 360-ff.
12. Francisco A. Encina, *History of Chile*, Vol. 16, pp. 113-131.
13. Galdames, *Op. Cit.*, p. 340.
14. Donoso, *Op. Cit.*, p. 287.
15. *Ibid.*, p. 214.
16. Domingo Santa Maria, *The Record*, June 21, 1884.
17. Robert E. Speer, *Studies of Missionary Leadership*, pp. 213-214.
18. *Ibid.*, p. 208.
19. *The Record*, "Banquet to the President," February 21, 1884, p. 8.
20. Galdames, *Op. Cit.*, pp. 340-341.
21. W. E. Dodge, *Letter to the Presbyterian Mission Board*, in Robert E. Speer's Studies of Missionary Leadership, pp. 211-212.

22. *Ibid.*, pp. 212-213.
23. *Political Constitution of the Chilean Republic;* Promulgated September 18, 1925, in conformity with the Official Edition. Also J. Lloyd Mecham, *Church and State in Latin America*, p. 269.

CHAPTER 10. *Mission Accomplished*

1. *The Record*, March 1889, pp. 8-9. "Sermon by the late Dr. David Trumbull."
2. David Trumbull, Yale University, "From the Class of 1842 Letter written June 12, 1887."
3. *Ibid.*
4. Robert E. Speer, *South American Problems*, p. 243.
5. J. M. Allis, *The Record*, February 23, 1889, p. 5.
6. *The Record*, February 23, 1889, pp. 19-20.
7. *El Heraldo*, February 2, 1889, quoted in *The Record*, Vol. 18, No. 291, February 23, 1889, pp. 21-22.
8. W. R. Wheeler, et.al., *Modern Missions in Chile and Brazil*, pp. 57-58. Also, James H. McLean, *Historia de la Iglesia Presbiteriana en Chile*, pp. 29-30.

CHAPTER 11. *Epilogue*

1. Jorge Mejia, *Biblical Renewal in Latin America*, pp. 208-209, from *Religious Dimension in the New Latin America*.
2. Manuel Larrain Errazuriz, *We Must Know the Signs of the Times*, quoted in John J. Considine, *The Religious Dimension in the New Latin America*, pp. 217-218.
3. Frederick B. Pike, *Church and State in Mid-Century Latin America*, pp. 16-17.
4. John A. MacKay, *The Spiritual Spectrum of Latin America*, p. 11.
5. Ignacio Vergara, *El Protestantismo en Chile*, p. 7.
6. *Ibid.*, p. 36.
7. *Ibid.*, p. 226.
8. W. E. Dodge, *The Record*, February 23, 1889, p. 10.
9. Eduardo Frei Montalva, from *Op. Cit., Religion, Revolution and Reform*, p. 37.

BIBLIOGRAPHY

CHAPTER 1. *The New England Heritage*

Calvinism and The Reformation

Bainton, Roland H., *The Reformation of the Sixteenth Century*. Boston: Beacon Press, 1952.
Harkness, Georgia, *John Calvin: The Man and His Ethics*. New York: Abingdon Press, 1931.
Kerr, Hugh Thomson, Jr., *A Compend of the Institutes of the Christian Religion - By John Calvin*. Philadelphia: The Westminster Press, 1939.
McNeill, John T., *The History and Character of Calvinism*. New York: Oxford University Press, 1967.
Spitz, Lewis W., *The Reformation: Material or Spiritual?* Lexington, Mass: D. C. Heath and Company, 1968.
Walzer, Michael, *The Revolution of the Saints: A Study in the Origins of Radical Politics*. Cambridge, Mass: Harvard University Press, 1965.
Whale, J. S., *The Protestant Tradition*. London: Cambridge University Press, 1960.

Puritanism

Carroll, Peter N., *Puritanism and the Wilderness*. New York: Columbia University Press, 1969.
Haller, William, *The Rise of Puritanism*. New York: Harper & Brothers, 1938.

Miller, Perry and Johnson, Thomas H., eds., *The Puritans*. New York: American Book Company, 1956.
Perry, Ralph Barton, *Puritanism and Democracy*. New York: Vanguard Press, Inc., 1938.
Schneider, Herbert Wallace, *The Puritan Mind*. Ann Arbor: The University of Michigan Press, 1930.
Wertenbaker, Thomas Jefferson, *The Puritan Oligarchy*. New York: Grosset & Dunlap, Charles Scribner's Sons, 1947.

Cultural Development in New England

Bainton, Roland H., *Collected Papers in Church History*, (Series Three), Chapter IV, *Christian Unity and Religion in New England*, pp. 212-290. Boston: Beacon Press, 1964.
Bushman, Richard L., *From Puritan to Yankee: Character and Social Order in Connecticut, 1690-1765*. Cambridge: Harvard University Press, 1967.
Clark, George L., *History of Connecticut--Its Peoples and Institutions*. New York: G. P. Putman's Sons, 1914.
Green, M. Louis, *The Development of Religious Liberty in Connecticut*. Boston: Houghton, Miffler & Co., 1905.
Mead, Sidney E., *The Lively Experiment: The Shaping of Christianity in America*. New York: Harper and Row, 1963.
Miller, Perry, *The New England Mind: From Colony to Province*. Boston: Beacon Press, 1953.
Trumbull, Benjamin, *A Complete History of Connecticut; Civil and Ecclesiastic--From the Emigration of the First Planters From England 1630 to 1764*. New Haven: Malty & Goldsmith & Co., 1818.
Walker, Williston, *A History of the Christian Church*, (Revised Ed. 1969), Chapter 15, American Protestantism in the Nineteenth Century. New York: Charles Scribner's Sons, 1959.

CHAPTER 2. *Family Portrait*

Armstrong, Robert G., *Historic Lebanon, Highlights of an Historic Town*. Danielson, Connecticut: Ingalls Printing Co., 1950.
Atwater, Anita, *My Saga*, Unpublished manuscript-Memories of the life of a granddaughter of David Trumbull, in the keeping of Mrs. H. H. Battin. White Plains, 1960.
Bainton, Roland H., Manuscript, *Student Life Under the Elms*. Unpublished Chapter of *Yale and the Ministry*. New York: Harper & Brothers, 1957.
Hall, William, *The Old Homes - "Cherry Lawn"*. Article published in The Elizabeth Daily Journal, July 15, 1873.

Hatfield, Edwin F., *History of Elizabeth Town, New Jersey*. New York: Carleton and Lanaker, 1868.
Speer, Robert E., *Studies of Missionary Leadership*. Philadelphia: The Westminster Press, 1914.
Stuart, I. W., *Life of Jonathan Trumbull 1786-1861*. Boston: Crocker & Brewster, 1859.
Trumbull, *The Record Book of the First Presbyterian Church of Elizabeth Town, New Jersey 1688-1966*, and *Inscriptions on Tombstones in the Burial Ground of the First Presbyterian Church 1664-1892*.
Trumbull, David, *Journals 1844-1884*. New Haven, Princeton and Valparaiso, Chile. In the keeping of his granddaughter Alice Trumbull.
_____, *The Record*. (ed.) Bi-monthly periodical. Valparaiso, Chile: 1871-1889.
Trumbull, Jane Wales Fitch, *Private Journal 1848-1850's*. In the keeping of Alice Trumbull, Valparaiso, Chile.
Trumbull, J. Hammond, (ed.), *The Memorial History of Hartford County, Connecticut, 1633-1884*. Boston: E. L. Osgood, 1886.
Trumbull, John, *Andean Melodies*. New York: The Knickerbocker Press, 1912.
_____, *Autobiography: Reminsences and Letters*, Revised Edition, Theodor Sizer (ed.). New Haven: Yale University Press, 1953.
Trumbull, William, *The Legend of the White Canoe*. New York: G. P. Putman's Sons, 1894.
Weaver, Glenn, *Jonathan Trumbull: Connecticut's Merchant Magistrate (1770-1785)*. Hartford: The Connecticut Historical Society, 1956.
Yale College, *Class of 1842 - Biographical Record*. New Haven, 1878. Class letters 1888, 1889. *History of the Class of 1880 - Biographies of Graduates*. *Biographical Sketches of Graduate Members, Quarter Centenary Record-Yale '78*.

CHAPTER 3. *The Education and Call to Service of David Trumbull*

Bainton, Roland H., *Yale and the Ministry - How a Puritan School Moulded Generations of Americans*. New York: Harper & Brothers, 1957.
Fisher, George P., *Life of Benjamin Silliman*. Vols. I & II. New York: Charles Scribner's Sons, 1866.
Goodsell, Fred Field, *They Lived Their Faith*. Boston: The American Board of Commissioners For Foreign Missions, 1961.
_____, *You Shall be My Witness. An Interpretation of the History of the American Board 1810-1960*. Boston: The American Board of Commissioners For Foreign Missions, 1959.

Hodge, A. A., *Life of Charles Hodge*. Princeton: Charles Scribner's Sons, 1880.
Princeton Theological Seminary, *Dossier for David Trumbull*.
_____, *General Catalogue, 1815-1858*. Princeton, New Jersey, 1858.
Stokes, Anson Phelps, *Memorials of Eminent Yale Men*. Vol. I and II. New Haven: Yale University Press, 1914.

CHAPTER 4. *Forerunners in the Vale of Paradise*

Adams, William, *Life and Service of Rev. John C. Brigham*. Discourse of the Pastor of Madison Square Presbyterian Church. New York: American Bible Society, 1863.
Alberdi, J. B., *Life of William Wheelwright in South America*. Tr. from Spanish by Caleb Cushing. Boston: Williams Press, 1877.
American Bible Society, *Agents in Partibus*. Essays based on reports of Colporteurs and Agents in Latin America, 1832-1841. New York.
Bilbao, Francisco, *El Evangelio Americano y Paginas Selectas*. Barcelona: Casa Editorial Maucci, 1903.
Browning, Webster E., *Joseph Lancaster, James Thompson, and the Lancasterian System of Mutual Instruction with Special Reference to Latin America*. Reprint of an article published in the Hispanic American Review. Lebanon, Pa; Sowers Printing Co., 1936.
_____, *The Romance of the Founding of Evangelical Missions in Latin America*. Unpublished Manuscript, a copy of which is in the United Presbyterian Church in the U.S.A. Mission Library. Buenos Aires, 1935.
Christian World, The, *Monthly Periodical of the Foreign Evangelical Society*. Established in 1839 and merged with the American Protestant Society and the Christian Alliance in 1849 to become The American and Foreign Christian Union. Volumes I-XXXIV.
Crawford, William Rex, *A Century of Latin American Thought*. Revised Edition. Cambridge: Harvard University Press, 1961.
Crow, John A., *The Epic of Latin America*. New York: Doubleday & Company, Inc., 1950.
Donoso, Armando, *El Pensamiento Vivo De Francisco Bilbao*. Santiago: Editorial Nascimento, 1940.
Donoso, Ricardo, *Las Ideas Políticas en Chile*. Mexico: Fondo de Cultura Economica, 1946.
Dwight, H. O., *Centenial History of the American Bible Society*. Volumes I and II. New York: The MacMillan Co., 1916.
Edwards, Alberto, *La Fronda Aristocrática*. Santiago: Editorial Del Pacifico S.A., 1952.

Hill, Henry, *Recollections of an Octogenearian.* Boston: P. Lothrop & Co., 1884.
Hillman, Charles F. (Quien Sabe), *Old Timers in Chile, British and American.* Santiago: Imprenta Moderna, 1900.
Latourette, Kenneth Scott, *Christianity in a Revolutionary Age.* Volumes I and III. New York: Harper & Brothers, 1958.
Missionary Herald, *Published for the American Board of Commissioners for Foreign Missions, New York.* Vol. XIX, Feb. 1823; Vol. XXII, Oct. 1826 and Nov. 1826.
Sailors' Magazine, *Periodical of the American Seamen Friend Society.* Organized in January, 1826. The Sailors' Magazine printed the Annual Reports of the Seaman Society and frequent letters from David Trumbull who organized the Valparaiso Seaman's Mission, January 4, 1846.
Salas, Eugenio Pereira, *Henry Hill - Comerciante, Vice-Consul y Misionero.* Santiago: Imprenta Universitaria, 1940.
Solar, Domingo Amunategui, *El Sistema de Lancaster en Chile y en Otros Paises Sud-Americanos.* Santiago: Imprenta Cervantes, 1895.

CHAPTER 5. *The Reformed Church in the Wilderness*

Arms, Goodsil F., *History of the William Taylor Self-Supporting Missions in South America.* New York: The Methodist Book Concern, 1921.
Brown, Aruthur Judson, *One Hundred Years.* New York: Fleming Revell Co., 1936.
Browning, Webster E., *What the Old Boys Say.* Santiago, Chile: Imprenta Universo, 1915.
_____, *The West Coast Republics of South America.* London: World Dominion, 1930.
Canton, William, *History of the British and Foreign Bible Society.* London: John Murry, 1910. (5 v.)
Erickson, Margaret Gilbert, *A Cross of Iron is His Tribute.* Letters and Notes of Nathaniel Gilbert. Private Publication, 1960.
Every, Bishop E. E., *The Anglican Church in South America.* London: Society for the Promoting of Christian Knowledge, 1915.
Galdames, Luis, *A History of Chile.* Tr. and ed. by I. J. Cox, Chapel Hill, North Carolina, 1941.
Hodgson, C. H., *Sketch of the Anglican Chaplaincy at Valparaiso, 1825-1909.* Valparaiso: South Pacific Mail, 1917.
Kessler, Jean Baptiste August, Jr., *A Study of the Older Protestant Missions and Churches in Peru and Chile.* Goes, Netherlands: Oosterbaan & Le Cointre, N.V., 1967.

Miller, Perry, *Errand Into the Wilderness*. Cambridge: Harvard University Press, 1956.
Oyarzun, Arturo, *Reminiscencias Historicas de la Obra Evangelica en Chile*. Valdivia, Chile: Imprenta Alianza, 1921.
Presbyterian Board of Foreign Missions, *Annual Report*, 1883 and 1889. Microfilms, Chile Correspondence 1872-1900, Vols. 31-43.
Strong, W. E., *Story of the American Board*. Boston: Pilgrim Press, 1910.
Vergara, Ignacio, *El Protestantismo en Chile*. Santiago: Editorial del Pacifico, 1962.
Wheeler, W. Reginald, and Speer, Robert E., *Modern Missions in Chile and Brazil*. Philadelphia: The Westminster Press, 1926.

CHAPTER 6. *Agent of the Evangelical Magisterium*

Chilean Times, *Biographical Sketch of David Trumbull*. August 4, 1888.
Donoso, Ricardo, *Las Ideas Politicas en Chile*. Mexico: Fondo de Cultura Economica, 1946.
Encina, Francisco Antonio, *Historia de Chile*. Volumes XII and XIV. Santiago: Editorial Nascimento, 1940-1952.
Evans, Oswald Hardey, *The Mackay School: An Outline of Its History 1857-1957*. Valparaiso: Imprenta Victoria, 1957.
Hunt, Wallis, *Heirs of Great Adventure: The History of Balfour, Williamson and Company Limited, 1851-1901*. Norwich, England: Jarrold and Sons Limited, 1960. (2 Volumes).
Labarca, Amanda H., *Historia de la Ensenanza en Chile*. Santiago: Imprenta Universitaria, 1939.
Record, The, January 5, 1884 and April 5, 1884, Valparaiso, Chile.

CHAPTER 7. *The Word of God is Spread Abroad*

American Bible Society, The, *Seventy-Third Report, 1889; Eighty-First Report, 1897*; and *Historical Records*.
Canton, William, *History of the British and Foreign Bible Society*. London: John Murry, 5 V., 1910.
Christian World, The, *February 1860* and *December 1877*.
Hillman, Charles F. (Quien Sabe), *Old Timers, British and Americans in Chile*. Santiago: Imprenta Moderna, 1900.
Hunt, Wallis, *Heirs of Great Adventure: The History of Balfour, Williamson and Company Limited, 1851-1901*. Norwich, England: Harrold and Sons Limited, 1960.

Record, The, *March 29, 1879; March 6, 1884;* and *March 11, 1887.*
Walker, Williston, *A History of the Christian Church.* Revised Edition, 1969. New York: Charles Scribner's Sons, 1959.

CHAPTER 8. *The Gospel in the Reformed Tradition*

Calvin, John, *The Institutes of the Christian Religion.* See Hugh Thompson Kerr, Jr., A Compend of the Institutes of the Christian Religion, by John Calvin. Philadelphia: The Westminster Press, 1939.
Galdames, Luis, *A History of Chile.* Tr. by Isaac Joslin Cox. Chapel Hill: University of North Carolina Press, 1941.
Herring, Hubert, *A History of Latin America: From the Beginning to the Present.* New York: Alfred A. Knopf, 2nd ed. revised 1967.
Mackay, John A., *The Presbyterian Way of Life: What it Means to Live and Worship as a Presbyterian.* New Jersey: Prentice-Hall, 1960.
Mecham, J. Lloyd, *Church and State in Latin America.* Chapel Hill, N.C.: University of North Carolina Press, 1934.
Pike, Frederick B., *Chile and United States Relations, 1880-1962.* Notre Dame: University of Notre Dame Press, 1963.
Record, The, *November 18, 1887; December 31, 1884;* and *February 23, 1889.*
Wheeler, W. Reginald, et.al., *Modern Missions in Chile and Brazil.* Philadelphia: Westminster Press, 1926.

CHAPTER 9. *Advocate of Constitutional Reforms*

Collier, William Miller, and Cruz, Guillermo Feliu, *La Primera Mision de Los Estados Unidos de America en Chile.* Santiago: Imprenta Cervantes, 1926.
Donoso, Ricardo, *Las Ideas Politicas en Chile.* Mexico: Fondo de Cultura Economica, 1946.
Encima, Francisco A., *Historia de Chile.* Vol. XVI. Santiago: Editorial Nascimento, 1940-1952.
Evans, H. C., *Chile and Its Relations With the United States.* University of Florida Press, 1927.
Galdames, Luis, *A History of Chile.* Tr. and ed. by I. J. Cox. Chapel Hill, North Carolina: University of North Carolina Press, 1941.

Graham, Maria, *Diary of a Residence in Chile, during the year 1822; and a Voyage from Chile to Brazil, in 1823.* London: Longman, Hurst, Dies, Orms, Brown and Green, 1824.
McLean, James H., *History of the Presbyterian Church in Chile.* Santiago: Escuela Nacional de Artes Graficas, 1954.
Mecham, J. Lloyd, *Church and State in Latin America.* Chapel Hill: University of North Carolina Press, 1934.
Record, The, *February 21, 1884; June 21, 1884; December, 1888,* and *March, 1889.*
Speer, Robert E., *Studies of Missionary Leadership.* Philadelphia: The Westminster Press, 1914.

CHAPTER 10. *Mission Accomplished*

McLean, James H., *Historia de la Iglesia Presbiteriana de Chile.* Santiago: Escuela Nacional de Artes Graficos, 1954.
Record, The, *February 23, 1889;* and *March, 1889.*
Speer, Robert E., *South American Problems.* New York: Student Volunteer Movement for Foreign Missions, 1912.
Yale University, Class of 1842, Class Letter of 1888 and 1889.

CHAPTER 11. *Epilogue*

Considine, John J. M. M., *The Religious Dimension in the New Latin America.* Notre Dame, Indiana: Fides Publishers, 1966. (Chapter 18, "We Must Know the Signs of the Times", Manuel Larrain Errazuriz: Biblical Renewal in Latin America, Jorge Mejia, Chapter 17).
D'Antonio, William, and Pike, Frederick B., *Religion, Revolution and Reform.* New York: Frederick A. Praeger, 1964.
Mackay, John A., *The Spiritual Spectrum of Latin America.* New York: Latin American Department, Division of Overseas Ministries, National Council of Churches of Christ in the U.S.A., Symposium, 1965.
Pike, Frederick B., *Church and State in Mid-Century Latin America.* Symposium on The Churches and the Changing Order in Latin America. New York: Symposium on the Churches and the Changing Order in Latin America, National Council of Churches in the U.S.A., 1965.
Shapiro, Samuel (ed.), *Cultural Factors in Inter-America Relations.* Notre Dame: University of Notre Dame Press, 1968.

Irven Paul was born of Armenian parents at Fresno, California on May 14, 1894. The early years of his childhood were spent in an orphanage at Vallejo, California.

In 1913 he graduated from Los Angeles High School and in 1920 he received his B.A. from the University of California. While at the University he was President of the Student Y.M.C.A.

During the First World War he was an officer in the 26th Yankee Division and served overseas.

In 1923 he received the B.D. degree from San Francisco Theological Seminary at San Anselmo, California. While at the Seminary he was a member of the Gospel Team, the Seminary Quartet, and of the Basketball and Football teams.

In May of 1923, he was married to Catharine F. Manny. During the years 1923-1943, Mr. and Mrs. Paul served in Chile, South America, as missionaries of the United Presbyterian Church in the U.S.A., engaged especially in Christian Education and the promotion of the activities of the churches of the Presbytery of Chile.

Mr. Paul spent two years as Student Pastor at the University of Concepción, Chile. He was one of the founders of the Evangelical Youth Movement, which was integrated with the Latin American Union of Evangelical Youth in 1944.

For six years Mr. Paul was secretary of the World Sunday School Association in South America, and in the interests of the Association, traveled extensively throughout the southern continent.

In 1929 he received the degree of S.T.M. from the Union Theological Seminary in New York. He studied at the Divinity School of the University of Chicago from 1937-1938.

During 1942-1943 he was Assistant Minister of the First Presbyterian Church in Brooklyn, New York. He was Acting Minister of the Congregational Church at Terryville, Connecticut from 1944-1945.

In 1946 Mr. Paul received the degree of Ph.D. from the Hartford Seminary Foundation. From 1947 to 1951 he served on the faculty of the Union Theological Seminary of Buenos Aires, Argentina. From 1952-1962 he was Professor of Latin American Studies at the Hartford Seminary Foundation. In 1970 Mr. Paul was Lecturer of Government and Politics in Latin America at Trinity College in Hartford, Connecticut.

For four years Mr. Paul served as Chaplain to the Spanish-speaking migrants in Pennsylvania, Massachusetts, and Connecticut, and was pastor of the Spanish-speaking congregation in Hartford from 1956 to 1960.

Mr. Paul was a member of the Committee on Co-operation in Latin America, a member of the North American Committee of the World Council of Christian Education, a trustee of the Hartford Seminary Foundation, a director of the Greater Hartford Council of the People-to-People Movement, and is a Fellow of the American Anthropological Association.

Dr. and Mrs. Paul have a daughter, Helen, born in 1928, and a son, Philip, born in 1934.

Cover Design by Marshall Licht
Performing Arts
Beverly Hills
Calif.